SHATTERED FORMS

SUNY Series in Aesthetics and the Philosophy of Art
Mary C. Rawlinson, editor

SHATTERED FORMS

Art Brut, Phantasms, Modernism

Allen S. Weiss

State University of New York Press

Published by
State University of New York Press, Albany

Printed in the United States of America

For information, address State University of New York Press, State University Plaza, Albany, N.Y., 12246

Production by Marilyn P. Semerad
Marketing by Fran Keneston

Library of Congress Cataloging-in-Publication Data

Weiss, Allen S., 1953-
Shattered forms: art brut, phantasms, modernism / Allen S. Weiss.
p. cm. — (SUNY series in aesthetics and the philosophy of art)
Includes bibliographical references.
ISBN 0-7914-1117-6. — ISBN 0-7914-1118-4 (pbk.)
1. Art brut. 2. Psychoanalysis and art. 3. Avant-garde (Aesthetics)—History—20th century. 4. Modernism (Art) I. Title. II. Series.
N7432.5.A78W44 1992
701'.05—dc20 91-36290
CIP

10 9 8 7 6 5 4 3 2 1

For my parents,
Lala and Leslie Weiss.

CONTENTS

PART II. OTHER MODERNISMS

LIST OF ILLUSTRATIONS

ACKNOWLEDGMENTS

All previously published works have been revised.

The Introduction contains material originally published in "Prefatory Remarks: Art Brut Occlusions:" in *Art & Text* 27 (1988); and "An Open Letter on Art Brut" in *Raw Vision* 2 (1989).

"The Primacy of Matter: Art Brut and Modernism," first appeared in *SubStance* (1991). Used by permission of the University of Wisconsin Press.

"In the Devil's Kitchen: The Dolls of Michel Nedjar" appeared in French in *Furor* 19–20 [Lausanne] (1990); a short version was published in *Sulfur* 26 (1990).

"Figurations and Disfigurations" appeared in the catalogue of the show *Portraits From the Outside,* ed. Simon Carr, Betsey and Sam Farber, Allen S. Weiss, at the Parsons School of Design Gallery, Fall 1990.

"The New Disfiguration" was first published in *Art & Text* 39 (1991).

"Outside In: On the Problem of Demarginalization" and "A New Anxiety of Influence" appeared in *Art & Text* 35 (1989).

"Art Therapy, Outreach, Art Brut" is previously unpublished.

"Écrits Bruts: The Other Scene of Writing" is previously unpublished.

"Music and Madness" was published in *Public* 4 [Toronto] (1991); a French version appeared as "La musique et la folie: Wolfson, Artaud, Wölfli," in *Furor* 21 (1991); the section on Wölfli also appeared in French in the catalogue to the exhibition *Wölfli: Dessinateur-Compositeur* (Lausanne: L'Age d'Homme, 1991).

"Kinomadness" is previously unpublished.

"Radiophonic Art: The Performance of the Impossible Body" appeared in *Discourse* (1992).

"Edible Architecture, Cannibal Architecture" was commissioned for the collective volume *Eating Culture*, edited by Ron Scapp and Brian Seitz.

The diagram in chapter 1, from Hans Prinzhorn, *Artistry of the Mentally Ill*, is used by permission of Springer-Verlag, Heidelberg.

INTRODUCTION

Invocation of a Different Art

Rimbaud, in a letter that remains one of the most celebrated statements of modern aesthetics, sets forth a hallucinatory, delirious poetics: "The poet makes himself a *visionary* through a long, a prodigious and rational disordering of all the senses. Every form of love, of suffering, of madness; he searches himself, he consumes all the poisons in him, keeping only their quintessences."[1] There exists a certain desire for poetic derangement and dissociation—nourished by the hyperbolic expressions of Romanticism and Symbolism, and inspiring both Expressionism and Surrealism—which marks an extreme limit of art. Here, the creative act is founded upon the linguistic and psychological dislocations needed to shatter the codes of everyday communication. Simulated delirium became the object of a new art—experimental, avant-garde, modernist—which arose from these fragmented codes, these shattered forms. But what of those artists whose works, and often whose deliria, are the manifestations of sheer eccentricity, of social isolation and marginalization, or of madness?

In our postmodern epoch, we might investigate the origins of the unrestricted contemporary artistic field, and seek one of its sources in those works hitherto absent from the official histories of art—works that constitute art's dark interior, its disturbing netherworld. Secluded, occluded, excluded, Art Brut nevertheless extends the limits of artistic creativity and aesthetic discourse, regardless of whatever anxieties such works may produce.

Michel Thévoz defined Art Brut, "not as *another culture*, but as *something other than culture*." Jean Dubuffet has insisted that Art Brut is in fact the true art, found where art forgets its very name. Dubuffet:

> We understand by this term works produced by persons unscathed by artistic culture, where mimacry plays little or no part (contrary

> to the activities of intellectuals) [. . .] We are witness here to a completely pure artistic operation, raw, brute, and entirely reinvented in all of its phases solely by means of the artists' own impulses.[2]

These works, also referred to as *Outsider Art,* must be distinguished from folk art, popular art, religious inspirational art, the creations induced by art therapy, and so forth—all of which are derivative from cultural artistic norms. Yet, realizing the ultimate impossibility of escaping the influence of culture—even in the most remote isolation, even in the most arcane thought, the most recondite realms of the imagination—Dubuffet modified his position by admitting that such works are characterized by countless hybrid nuances, and that the notion of "Art Brut" is an aspiration rather than a definition, a tendency rather than a style or a category, a direction rather than a place.[3]

Yet today, Art Brut has its own museums and curators, galleries and dealers, journals and writers, hospital archives and psychotherapeutic specialists. Indeed we are in a pivotal historic moment: Art Brut is on the verge of becoming assimilated by "official" art history. Dubuffet's own artistic productions, themselves often simulacra of Art Brut, were destined for the museum, and they eventually dragged Art Brut in along with them. What was once a marginal art (a sort of ante- or alter-art) is fast becoming assimilated. We must realize, though, that our studies of Art Brut reveal not only our participation in a new chapter of its history, but even more so tell a tale of our own phantasms, our own passions expressed in an increasingly idealized form. We can only attempt to disclose some of the discursive, polemical and historical substructures of this idealization, all the while remembering that we must not permit theory to dissimulate the role of polemic. We must hope for that subtle shift of motives, so central to contemporary thought, which entails the presentation of theory *as* polemic, polemic as history, history as criticism, criticism as theory.

Ultimately, the present project finds its motives in a disquieting strangeness felt at certain margins of art—indeed, at the margins of Art Brut itself—at this historical juncture where both such margins and such strangeness are in danger of extinction, or at least of oblivion. We seek not so much a new mode of expiatory dejection or radical subversion as we do the oldest form of appreciation: fascination. Thus we might permit ourselves the luxury of a certain nostalgia—an active, critical nostalgia—insofar as it may signal the delineations of a project, a projection, of our own passions, precisely there where they intersect with the unexpected, unavowed, unnamed passions of those others . . .

As is the case with all attempts at "enlightenment," rationalization entails a certain degree of domination. Following Foucault, we have learned to think according to a philosophy of suspicion, calling into question institutionalization and categorization, but equally interrogating all attempts to naively circumvent bureaucracies and escape hierarchies. The history of our century has taught us that fascination may entail the aestheticization of politics leading to fascism, and nostalgia may be a major device of reaction. Our jubilatory modes of aesthetic appreciation must be tempered by a critique of the utilization and destiny of aesthetic objects.

Dubuffet's project (already appropriated by the "establishment") and his polemic (already outmoded by an all-encompassing "postmodernism") was founded on his own fascination with a certain *difference*. This Art Brut difference, which bears madness as only one of its aspects, was traditionally projected outside of ourselves, our cultures, our art. Dubuffet taught us that, in fact, such aesthetic alterity is always to be found within ourselves, and must be cultivated. Dubuffet's project, ambiguously expressed and rhetorically overbearing, may serve as a performative introduction to this domain of "suppressed knowledge," but not as its ultimate analysis or definition.

In a sense, the constant refinement of categories, the harsh vigilance in guarding the boundaries of Art Brut, and the infinite regression of differentiations based on "borderline" cases, are all refusals of vision, denials of thought. If we are to be concerned with the contradictions inherent in such works, let these be the contradictions of their material production and not the empty conundrums of categorical motives or aesthetic imperatives. If Art Brut is truly *brut,* "raw," then we must be attuned to the differences, particularities and individualities that this term signifies. Although it may be *brut,* it is certainly not without history.

But even furthermore, we must always be attentive to the fragility of Art Brut, due precisely to the ephemeral nature of such works. Yet why should some art not be ephemeral, why should some works not disappear, like the sand castles on the beaches of our childhood or the golden palaces and hellish grottos of our dreams? This fragility is also evident in the very lives of their creators, many of whom, marginalized in our psychiatric institutions, lead the most fragile existence in the most harsh climate, themselves ephemera in relation to the rest of our culture. These people are always on the very of becoming not *unheimlich,* but literally homeless, totally dispossessed. Yet if certain creators of Art Brut wish to remain silent, isolated, secretive, if they wish to hide or destroy their own works, why should we not acquiesce? These considerations must necessarily go beyond aesthetics, whence the ethical imperative of Art Brut. Many such works (especially those originating in psychiatric hospitals) are expressions of pain, attempts at communication, cries of recognition—as well as productions of art. It is precisely this suffering that is often forgotten by those who otherwise valorize such art. Pain, the memories of pain, or the overcoming of pain is transformed into meaningful signs of the relation of the creator's body to the socius. When these artists do wish to communicate, we must take up their signs as our own, by giving voice to those who otherwise have so little chance to gain an audience.

In reconsidering these works of Art Brut, as well as their multifarious effects on the modernist artistic enterprise, we must ask ourselves—beyond our fascination with otherness and difference, beyond our nostalgia for the origins of creativity and aesthetic purity—precisely how we wish to use these works and what we wish to establish as their fate. We must ultimately ask whether any difference, once expressed and examined, can maintain its otherness. And we might just recognize that these others, whose dreams and phantasms seem so different from our own, are but our very doubles, whose alterity founds our culture, our art, our selves.

Part I.
Art Brut

ONE

The Primacy of Matter: Art Brut and Modernism

> In the primordial mud of existence, an exhumed doll, a miraculated body soaked with tears.
>
> —*Michel Nedjar*

The sites of aesthetic discovery are as varied as our passions and our fears. The objects of our fascination, the raw matter of our arts, are sometimes familiar and reassuring, sometimes bizarre and uncanny. Sometimes such things lead us back to our childhood, sometimes forward to the moment of our death. On certain rare occasions, birth and death are conflated, and we are privy to the internal workings of the cosmos, revealing the very origins of our being.

In *Nadja* (1928), André Breton recounted that he would often go to the flea market at Saint-Ouen, just outside of Paris: "I go there often, searching for objects that can be found nowhere else: old-fashioned, broken, useless, almost incomprehensible, even perverse."[1] These *objets trouvés* [found objects] are emblematic of the Surrealist aesthetic: manifestations of "objective chance," they not only correspond to the dreams of the *flaneur* who discovers them, but they furthermore create reveries, that key feature of Surrealist poetics.

In the already standardized commercial culture of Paris in the 1920s, the flea market was the rare place where such found objects, whether *objets naturels* or *objets perturbés,* might still be discovered.

Once recycled in the context of the flea market, these objects—the refuse of history—are disposed in a sort of unorganized, unconscious collage, a mixture of epochs, places and styles where the centuries collide and exotic cultures infiltrate our own. The attraction, as Breton explained in *L'amour fou,* where he told of yet another trip to the same flea market in 1934, this time with Alberto Giacometti, is that of the *jamais vu* [the never seen], of the absolutely unique and unknown.[2] Such "oneiric" objects play the role of a poetic catalyst, where the structure of the imagination becomes a function of the aesthetic derealization of the everyday world, leading toward the re-creation of the cosmos as thoroughly marvelous.

Jean Dubuffet too frequented the flea markets of Paris, but for quite different purposes, albeit ultimately aesthetic ones. In his article "Saint-Ouen—Le Marché" [1944], he told of his fascination with this place. But rather than vaunt the rare, the unusual, the marvelous, his is a celebration of the commonplace, of "man settled into his presence, fully accessible, a radiously open mold [. . .] Man, oh my feast!"[3]

Briefly after founding *La compagnie de l'Art Brut,* dedicated to collecting those works of Art Brut (created by the insane, the eccentric, the isolated), which Dubuffet initially saw as stemming from the impulses of the common man, untainted by cultural conventions, Dubuffet took yet another trip to the flea market at Saint Ouen (June 1948). This time he went at the suggestion of André Breton (one of the charter members of the *compagnie*), to purchase some of Maisonneuve's masks that Breton had discovered there [figure 1]. Unlike for Breton, these voyages were not primarily inspired by the search for the unknown, but were rather motivated by the project of collecting objects of Art Brut—objects as marvelous as any that Breton had previously discovered. And yet, these trips would have another effect: it is precisely the banal textures and forms, objects and images of the everyday world that Dubuffet would ultimately recuperate into his own works of art, into his own aesthetic.

Dubuffet's radical attraction to pure, unadulterated, base matter is allegorically exemplified in a letter to his friend Jacques Berne: "I was enchanted by the crayfish, which pleased me greatly, and I thank you. It is a very rich food. Almost too rich. Too rich! I often tell Lili that her cooking is too rich—cream, butter, etc. I much prefer grass, or earth, which seems to me to be much more sumptuous. To eat earth, now there's a rich dish!"[4] He was equally explicit about the use of diverse

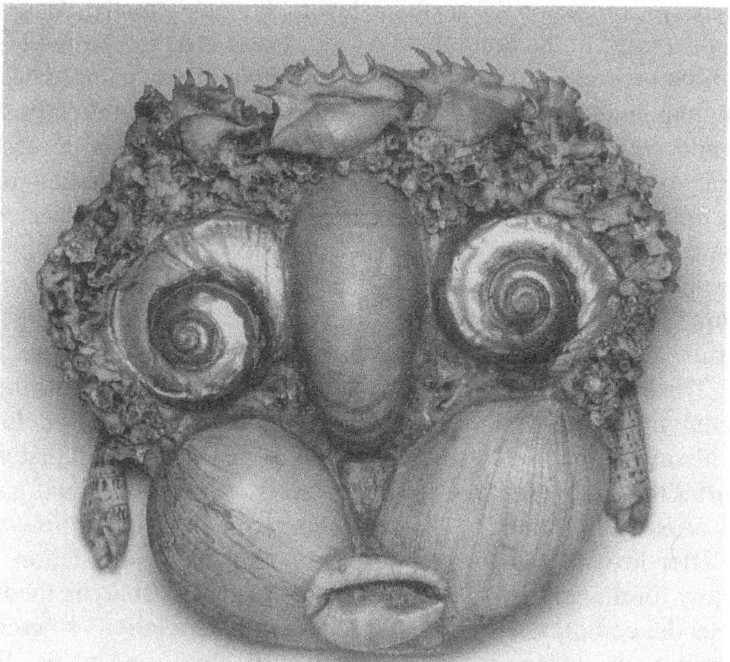

Figure 1. Pascal Maisonneuve, "The Eternal Infidel," 1928 (photo courtesy the Collection de l'Art Brut, Lausanne).

matières primaires on the aesthetic level: "It would greatly please me to use cow dung. In the Sahara, when the Arabs have something to putty or a hole to stop up, they use a paste formed by kneading dates with goat dung and a bit of sand. That's an ingredient which greatly moves me, and which I fully expect to use one day."[5] Here is an aesthetic desire working against itself, moving toward an antiaesthetic—or perhaps more accurately a counteraesthetic—procedure. In other words, Dubuffet proposes what amounts to a desublimatory aesthetic in opposition to the sublimatory exigencies of what he refers to as the *cultural arts*. (And these arts most certainly included Surrealism.) Such a desublimation is evident in his celebration of pure living matter itself.

This materiological, indeed scatological, aesthetic recalls the psychoanalytic understanding about the origins of the artwork. Lexical considerations are highly revelatory in this regard: we learn that *matter* signifies the "indeterminate ground of being," the chaotic, unorganized stuff of existence; and by ellipsis, *matter* can signify *fecal matter*[6]—this latter lexical transformation, or euphemistic dissimulation, is an allegory for the process of sublimation itself. Psychoanalytic theory describes the complex set of unconscious symbolic relations whereby for the infant, the feces are equated with gift, child, and penis. Excrement—as pure formless matter, as pure body—functions as both good and bad object, as gift or weapon. Infantile play with the feces prefigures the artistic activity of sculptural production. In the process by which the infant is socialized, the first exclusion demanded of the individual body by the body politic is that of excrement: simultaneously the sign of our guilt (bad object, weapon, stain) and the sign of our power (good object, gift, magical talisman, artwork). Here, all nonproductive expenditure is abolished and dissimulated in the symbolic machine of cultural activity. This exclusion, this destruction of our primal sovereignty, is the very origin of sublimation. Excrement—as an image of death, as pure, formless, heterogeneous matter—is excluded from the symbolic order. All culture is the sublimation of this primal creative activity; and as anality is the mark of death, all sublimation is somehow the projection of the instinctual life of the repressed body into dead things, into cultural artifacts. Desublimation is achieved in those rare instances when adult social production takes the inverse route back toward the body, breaking the significative chain of quotidian existence by inaugurating a return of the repressed. In moving toward such dark, asymbolic doubles, the long-repressed horror of death is revealed as the underside of the instincts, desires, and culture.[7]

We find the limits of scatological creativity in certain Art Brut creations of the mentally ill. Note the work of Georgine Hu (found in the museum L'Aracine), a patient in a psychiatric hospital just outside of Paris.[8] Her art consists of false banknotes created on toilet paper, with which she often attempted to pay her psychiatrist! Here, the scatological significance of money, the link between excrement and filthy lucre, is symbolized in a desublimated creativity, where the black humor and irony of the situation call into question both the economic and psychological aspects of creativity as well as all psychiatric endeavors. But it is not only in the art of the mentally ill that expression rediscovers its primal, scatological, corporeal component.

If Dubuffet's art was indeed influenced by those creations of Art Brut that he collected, it was more so in terms of the use of inhabitual materials and techniques than regarding formal innovations. Indeed, Dubuffet's entire artistic enterprise was more concerned with material than formal causes and effects. Michel Thévoz explained in his detailed study, *Dubuffet,* the contrast between the formal and material characteristics of art: "Matter, to the contrary, is the immediate, the unformed, the unnameable, what has neither identity nor determinations nor the civil status of Being. It does not lend itself to differentiation or to organization or to delimitation; or, what amounts to the same thing, it lends itself to all this much too complaisantly."[9] Dubuffet's varied series of works—*Texturologies, Topographies, Géographies, Matériologies, Pâtes Battues*—all exemplify his passion with raw matter by proffering pure textures without representational significance. But in fact, all of his work is a celebration of matter. Such "inspiration" by matter is the ultimate localization and particularization of the aesthetic object, hence the ultimate degree of antiinfluence. It is an aesthetic detotalization, where signifier and signified are perpetually conflated, and where artistic creativity is closest to its material, and thus cosmological, origins.

This opposition of matter to form—with pure matter as zero-degree form—leads directly to the problematic of the formless in art. This issue was already evident in modernist discourse, being at the core of the rupture in the Surrealist movement around 1930, especially in the polemic between André Breton and Georges Bataille.[10] Breton's poetic, idealized, sublimated mode of art was criticized by Bataille as being "pretentious idealist aberrations" and "nauseating utopian sentimentality." In opposition to Breton's dialectical idealism, Bataille proposed a sort of nondialectical materialism, a desublimatory heterology guided by sovereign wasteful expenditure, by transgression and excess. This position was implicitely an antiaesthetic, as exemplified by Bataille's dictionary entry in the journal *Documents* for the word *informe* [formless], which ends with the claim: "affirming that the universe resembles nothing and is only *formless* amounts to saying that the universe is something like a spider or spit."[11]

Dubuffet too broke with Breton, in 1951, though for very different reasons than Bataille (related to the dissolution of the *Compagnie de l'Art Brut);* Dubuffet's artistic position was also diametrically opposed to that of Breton. In that same epoch, Dubuffet spoke of his own work in terms of an *informisme, véhémentisme,* and *éclaboussurisme,*[12] and one of his earliest written texts, "Notes pour les fins-lettrés" [1946], begins with the subheading: "Partant de l'informe,"[13] where he argued that pure material itself is in fact already a language. Dubuffet also stressed the importance of chance as a function of the particularities of the materials employed in the artwork.[14] Whence the role of aberrations in the work of art: much later, Dubuffet would generalize these notions and claim that art itself is "a department of aberrations."[15]

The tradition of discovery in the context of the flea market continues today in Paris, manifested in the life and works of the artist Michel Nedjar. But unlike Breton and Dubuffet, who were finally only visitors to that place, Nedjar is integrally involved in the flea market at Clignancourt. Nedjar's maternal grandmother was a ragpicker [chiffonière]; his father, a tailor; he himself was trained to be a tailor and designer, yet abandoned this profession to travel, discover himself, and create his art; finally earning his living by working in the flea market several days a week. In his own words:

> My maternal grandmother used to buy up old clothes from middle-class homes. She would sell them at the Malik market. They were the *schmates*. The great times of the 50s. She was a ragpicker . . .
>
> The *schmate* really *was* my granny. In her shop, she would bury herself in them, she had them all over her and all around her; it was her whole life. She was completely crazy about them, she lived on them: old rags. She would never throw out the slightest

> scrap, or if anyone else did, she would go and recover it from the garbage bin, saying: "I'm sure I can get a price for this *schmate*."
>
> It's grandmother for the fabrics and father for the needlework which pulls the pieces together. The ragpicker and the tailor: it's strange how I combined those two things, to give birth to a little creature. The dolls I make are really their child: the central point where my grandmother's and my father's energies flow together.[16]

We find here the biographical foundation of Nedjar's aesthetic, the very *matière primaire* of his art. The sources of his artistic material are both the flea market, where he found much of the rags that he transformed into art, and an even more primal source of waste material, garbage cans.

> Continuity: because I never throw out any rags—that would be cruel—I risk being immersedalthogether. Every week I bring them home from the flea market. The solution I've found is to transform them. A rebirth through my work with old rags.
>
> For me, the garbage bin has something magical about it. It's so beautiful, the inside of a garbage bin, all those things gleaming up at you.[17]

Nedjar spoke of "the nostalgia of worn fabric," of the fact that, "the *schmate* is not an appearance; already it's closer to death, wearing out, old age. When it starts to glisten."[18] Beyond the collage aesthetic of the Cubists, beyond Duchamp's antiaesthetic of the "ready-made," beyond the found object aesthetic of the Surrealists, and beyond Dubuffet's radical celebration of a newly created "materiology," Nedjar's work, especially the dolls, entails the total resuscitation of waste material into the art object. [figures 2–6]. Yet this is an object that maintains its specific material and formal relations to the once abandoned rags, earth and waste matter of which it is made, all the while becoming a new sort of mythical, magical entity.

The title of one of Dubuffet's texts is, "Réhabilitation de la boue" (1946). If mud were ever "rehabilitated" in the history of art, it is in the work of Michel Nedjar:

> If I were to bury my dolls, it would be in order to dig them up again. The emotion of things decaying. Decaying material, the way the earth sets to work, the earth gnawing away, the mouldiness. The doll is transformed just as the body is undoubtedly transformed beneath the earth. For me, there is no frontier between

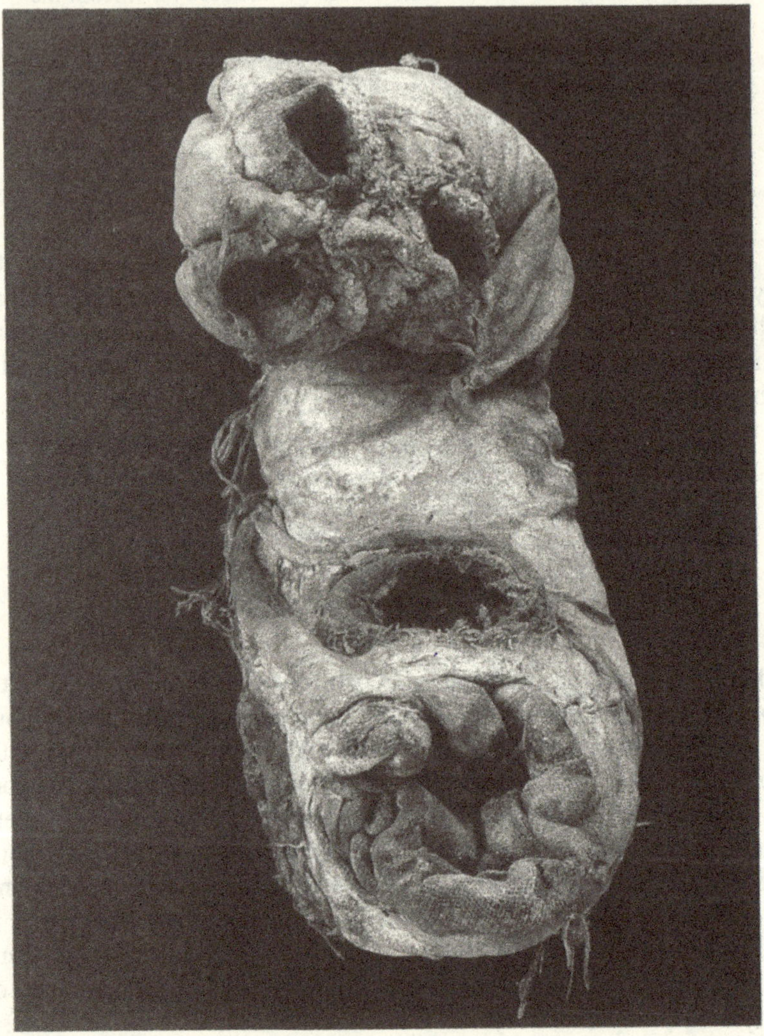

Figure 2. Michel Nedjar, "Doll" (photo Béatrice Hatala, courtesy Galerie Le Gall Peyroulet).

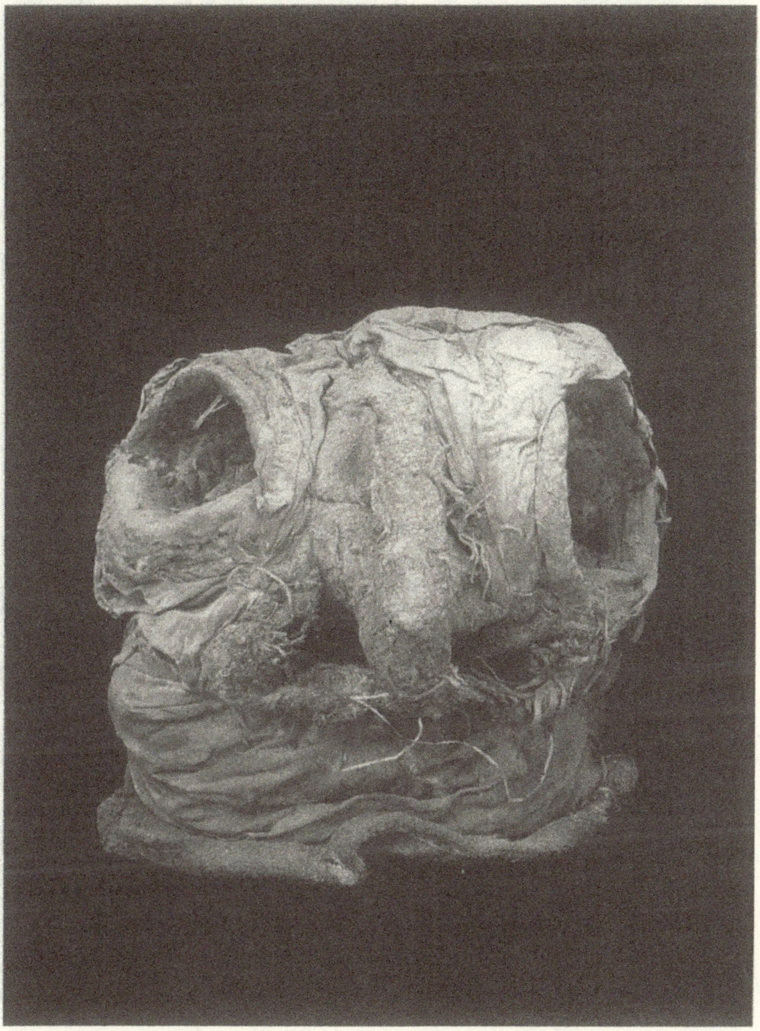

Figure 3. Michel Nedjar, "Mask" (photo Béatrice Hatala, courtesy Galerie Le Gall Peyroulet).

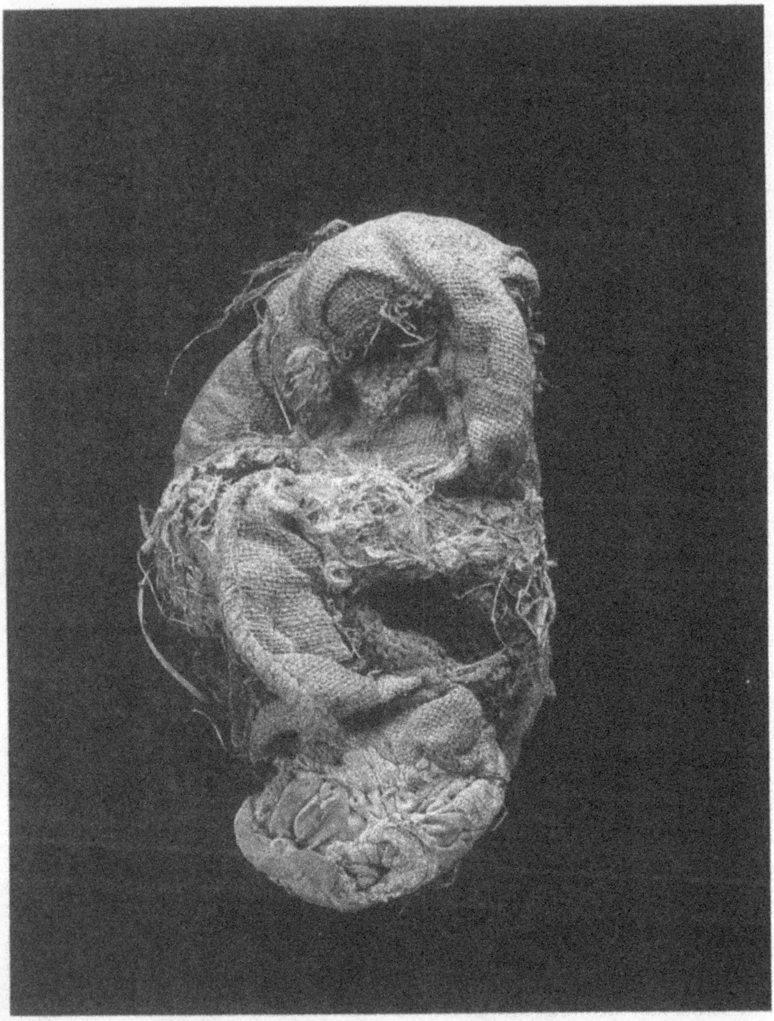

Figure 4. Michel Nedjar, "Mask" (photo Béatrice Hatala, courtesy Galerie Le Gall Peyroulet).

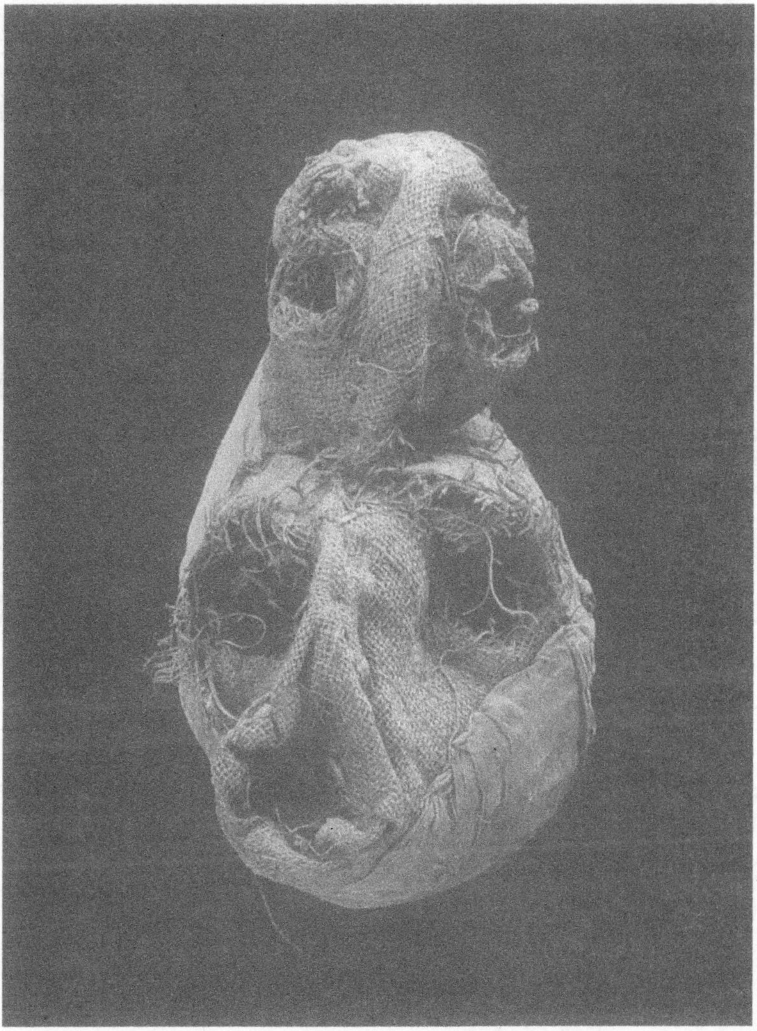

Figure 5. Michel Nedjar, "Mask" (photo Béatrice Hatala, courtesy Galerie Le Gall Peyroulet).

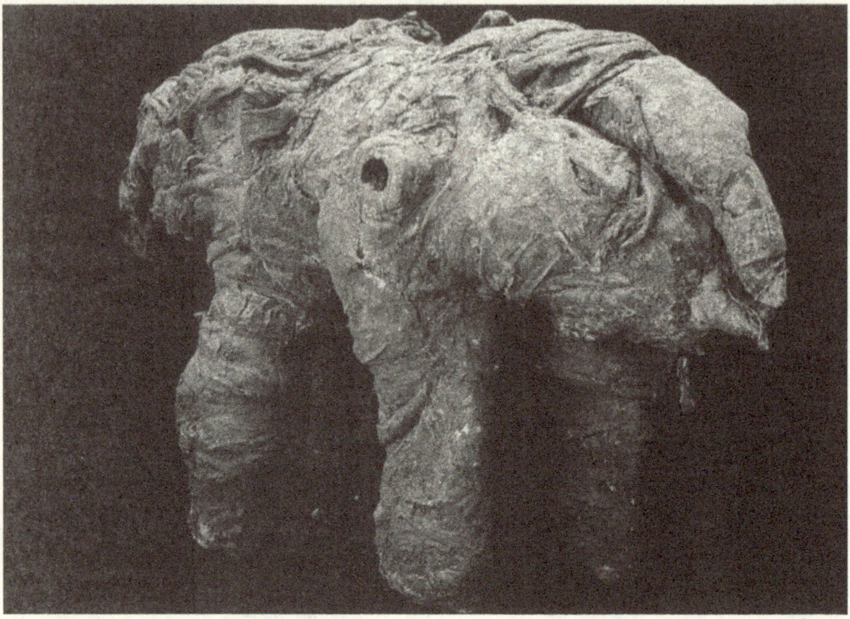

Figure 6. Michel Nedjar, "Animal" (photo David Boeno, courtesy Galerie Le Gall Peyroulet).

> decay and its opposite. I need a full transformation. I use cold dyes. That's the effect which the earth would have produced, and it's the effect that I achieve by putting it on the fabrics. Because I touch; I make a dough. It resembles mud.[19]

For Nedjar, the *matière primaire* of his art is identified with terra firma, especially in its amorphous state of mud; literally, "la nostalgie de la boue." Mud, shit, and blood: these are the sources of both life and art for Nedjar.

> The dolls represent the beginning of the world: they are animal, stone, woman, man, the universe—the primeval fundamental material. That's an extraordinary experience. It was terrible and at the same time extraordinary. I covered my dolls over with soil and blood and it was a very powerful thing—I thought I was going mad.[20]

In short, as Nedjar claims: "What's dirty is alive."[21] Or as Dubuffet insists: "Mud, refuse, and filth: these are man's lifelong companions. Shouldn't they be quite dear to him, and wouldn't it be doing him a favor to remind him of their beauty."[22]

Thinking back to Bataille's choice of the spider to symbolize the unformed, we can understand in part why Michel Nedjar chose the spider as his personal symbol. (It appears as the "star" of one of his films, *A quoi rêve l'araignée?* [1981–1982]; a plastic spider is to be found among his collection of magic dolls [figure 7]; its image protects the entranceway to his apartment; and it adorns his letters and postcards in the form of a rubberstamped image.) As the symbol of the unformed at the root of all formations (i.e., the ugly, terrifying spider spinning the archetypal natural aesthetic form, its beautiful web), as the chaos at the core of the cosmos, the spider symbolizes primal matter and creativity, as well as ultimate death.

Yet the difference between Nedjar and Dubuffet are apparent: whereas for Dubuffet the celebration of matter is ultimately a pragmatic means of discovering new effects (be they aesthetic or antiaesthetic), for Nedjar matter has a magical, even mystical quality. Despite occasional superficial formal similarities, it would be more precise to say that Nedjar's relation to Dubuffet is to be found on deeper levels. First, both of their oeuvres instantiate the hyperbolic instance of the modernist quest for accentuating the materiality of the artwork. (Though every artist is somehow concerned with the materials at hand, most dissimulate the material base of the work in favor of its formal effects). Sec-

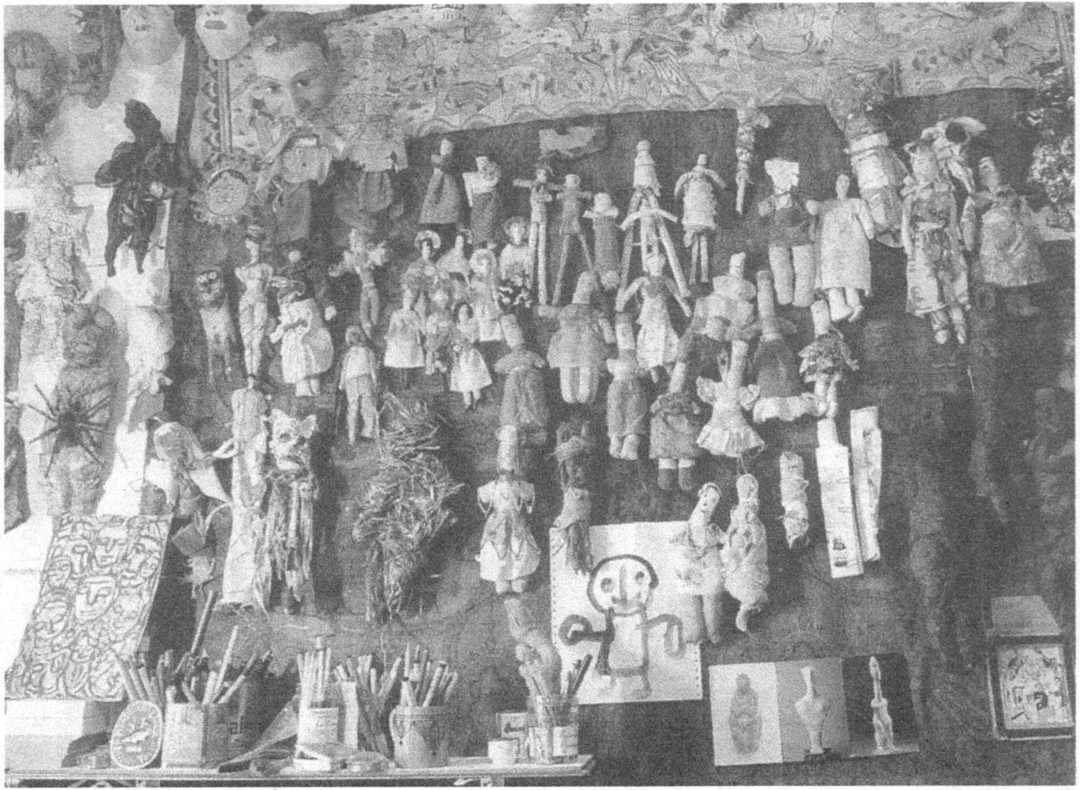

Figure 7. The doll collection of Michel Nedjar (photo Pascal Martin).

ond, it may be said that Dubuffet, who in fact chose Nedjar's dolls for inclusion in the *Collection de l'Art Brut* at Lausanne, was the first artist whose "tradition" was constituted by the heterogeneous nontradition of Art Brut. Michel Nedjar, who is a cofounder of *L'Aracine,* France's first museum of Art Brut, can also be said to have engaged Art Brut as his own tradition, once he discovered certain formal, material, and spiritual affinities between his own work and that of many Art Brut creators.

Yet this fascination with material is in fact directly related to the need for expression. Perhaps we may ascertain the very origins of art in the nexus of zero-degree matter and zero-degree expression. *Artistry of the Mentally Ill* is among the most influential studies of the art of the mentally ill, which by extention has also revealed the mainsprings of art in general, beyond the restricted realm of the psychopathology of expression. Here, Hans Prinzhorn described the crucial, central role of scribbling in the creative act. Scribbling is understood to be the key structural feature underlying the expressive gestalt of all artistic forms (see Figure 1.1).

These "unobjective disordered scribblings" bear a chronological and structural primacy within expression: not yet a "language," such pure expressive traces are signs of corporeal activity, limited by the very nature of the materials at hand. (And we might add that, mutatis mutandis, this schema also pertains to the most basic sculptural activity.) A fundamental, preformal figuration of the psychic gestalt, their expressive efficacy is lost as soon as the world is thematized, as soon as the world is categorized and denominated through the mimetic formalization of objects. These figurations then become the prime formal features of the artwork, within representational schemes of resemblance and appearance. Thus, even if matter itself is a language as Dubuffet claimed, there is a primal moment of creativity at which we still cannot quite speak through it. Here, it is the body that "speaks"; here the troubled, awkward, undexterous gesture paradoxically manifests an adequate expression of the spirit.

Dubuffet—whose final series of works, *Mires* (1983–1984) and *Non-Lieux* (1984), were a return to scribbled forms—was always concerned with what Thévoz referred to as our "psychic prehistory": "The plane surface, the stroke that is repeated, the form that is drawn, are all foreign to the natural world. They are not constitutively

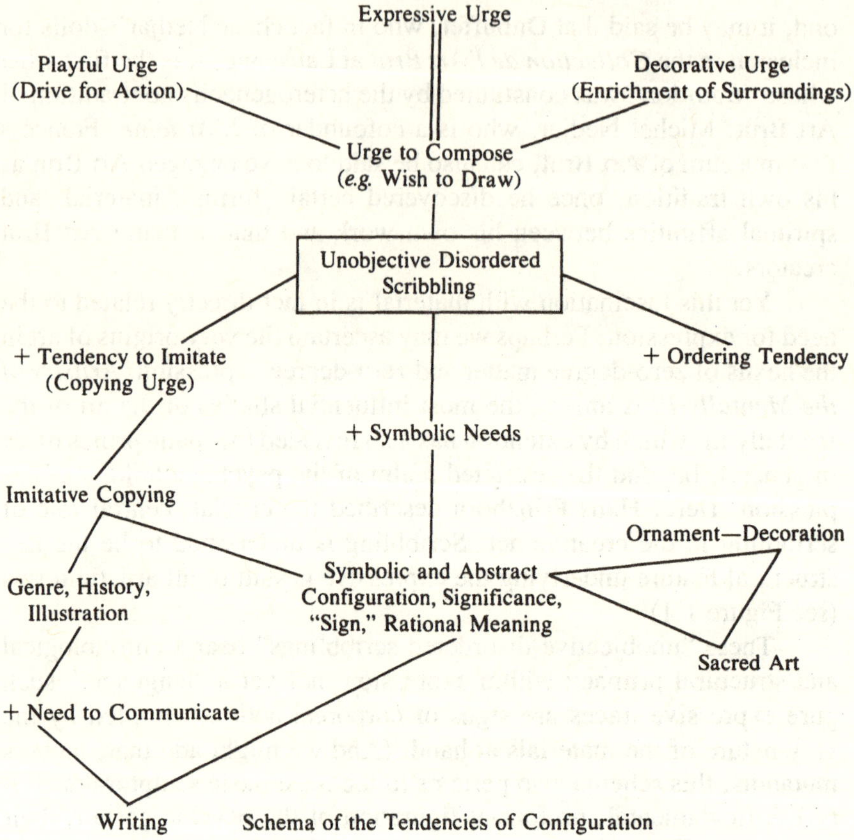

Figure 1.1. Schema of the Tendencies of Configuration

Source: Hans Prinzhorn, *Artistry of the Mentally Ill* [1922], English translation (Berlin: Springer-Verlag, 1968), p. 14.

devoted to mimetic representation; they only open up the symbolic register in its antefigurative polyvalence."[23] And as Dubuffet explains his own project:

> My apparatus functions as a machine to abolish the names of things, to collapse the walls that the mind sets up between diverse objects, between diverse systems of objects, between the different registers of facts and of things and the different planes of thought; a machine to scramble the entire order instituted by the mind within the walls of phenomena, and to erase with a single stroke all

> the paths traced out there; a machine to defeat all reason and to reinvest all things with equivocation and confusion.[24]

It is precisely these deformations stemming from expression—yet guided by the contingencies of matter—that effect a transformation of the aesthetic field. Dubuffet consciously puts these effects to work in constituting an antiaesthetic art, a contestation of the established modernist aesthetic domain. Yet this project remains sublimatory, even if only in the profoundly dialectical relation between cultural art and Dubuffet's antiart. To the contrary, Nedjar profited from a fascination with matter and the traces left by de-formative gestures to engender a desublimatory creation: anterior in time (his dolls harken back to the first playthings of childhood); regressive in matter (using the primordial mud, blood and excrement of mythopoeic creation, as well as working with his ancestral materials of rags); reclusive in space (secluded in his atelier, yet influenced by magical dolls from around the world; i.e., by arts whose formal aspects are ultimately subservient to their sacred potential).

In *La terre et les rêveries de la volonté,* Gaston Bachelard revealed the imaginary and symbolic relations between human creativity and the earth. In a chapter entitled "La pâte," he recounted a dream from Hans Carossa's book, *Une enfance*:

> In a *nighttime dream,* recounted at length, the book's hero sees an uncle appear who tells him point-blank: "Are you there, master modeler?" And the uncle places "three pellets of a reddish white mixture" in the hand of the young dreamer, suggesting that he "make a beautiful child."
>
> We should immediately understand that from the beginning of this oneiric story we are in the presence of the archetype of matter. These three pellets are really the primitive loam, the primal earth, the necessary and sufficient matter needed to "make a beautiful child." To create—in the strong sense of the word—is to create a child. In the dream, words often find their profound anthropomorphic sense. Besides, we should note that unconscious modeling is not of things, but of animals. A child, left to himself, makes a chicken or a rabbit. He creates life.
>
> But the dream works quickly; the sleeping modeler soon ends his oneiric tale: "I worked and kneaded the dough for a while, and suddenly held in my hand a marvellously beautiful little man." The *kneaded homonculus* will no doubt incite facile psychoana-

> lytic commentaries. But for us, as the rest of the tale will prove, it is here the sign of a profound aesthetic impulse.[25]

This tale might serve as an allegory for the creations of Michel Nedjar, works also born from a family drama, in the direct lineage of his father and maternal grandmother. Yet rather than learning to create by modeling, Nedjar needed to learn how to "unsew," as he says, in order to produce his dolls.

In a totally different context, the philosopher Maurice Merleau-Ponty, in developing an ontology of the human body, explained that the body is "that strange object which uses its own parts as a general system of symbols for the world."[26] This is a theory of sublimation. Conversely, we might say that for Michel Nedjar, the symbols and matter of the world are those strange entities that he used to form his specific representations, indeed deformations, of the human body—his dolls. This is a process, a poetics, of desublimation. And yet, their ultimate effect depends on whether we consider them to be merely art or something else, something closer to our own doubles, to the hidden side of our soul.

TWO

In the Devil's Kitchen: Morbidity and Memory

> The base of profound feelings.
> From the night arises the
> inexplicable, the undetailed,
> what is attached to visible
> causes, surprise attacks,
> mystery, the religious,
> fear . . . and monsters, which
> emerge from nothingness, not
> from a mother.
>
> —*Henri Michaux*
> *Emergencies-Résurgences*

There is an art of memory through which we may discern the order of the universe. Such an *ars memorativa,* or mnemotechnics, is a system whereby a set of images or words is constructed to aid in remembering another such set. The first set is used as the signifier of the second, or signified, set; thus, as Umberto Eco explained, mnemotechnics is a semiotics.[1] We also wish to show how mnemotechnics is a poetics.

Similarity often reigns in remembrance; yet it has long been known that, given a certain description, anything may be expressed as being similar to anything else. Similitude far surpasses the rhetorical function of metaphoricity and the poetic function of iconicity. Thus anything can be the sign of anything else. Within this inferential and connotative matrix, the ultimate limits of such a technique of free association would be a labyrinthine construction as complex as the universe itself, such that remembrance would be destroyed. As Eco explained: "Thus at the very center of a metaphysics of the correspondence between the order of representation and the order of the cosmos one is witness to a kind of theater of deconstruction and of infinite regress."[2] This would necessitate an "interpretive hermeticism," which is most certainly a rather cumbersome aid to memory. Here, idiosyncrasy would rule over tradition, and the past would be lost within the maze of the imagination. A simpler, more stable and codified system is needed.

Traditionally, the most elaborate form of such mnemonic devices consists of the establishment of a system of *loci* (places) in which we are to situate the images of things or words to be remembered. If memory is the shadow of order and order is the syntax of the universe, then it is not surprising that numerous mnemonic systems of Medieval influence utilized the diagram of the spheres of the universe or the signs of the zodiac as visual aids to artificial memory. The *imago mundi,* a pictorial representation of the cosmos itself, becomes the imaginary theater of memory within which we place what is to be remembered.[3] (Later on in the tradition, the "theater" of memory is literally represented as a sort of generic theater, within which the objects of memory are staged. The most famous of these are the sixteenth century "memory theater" of Giulio Camillo and the seventeenth century "theater memory system" of Robert Fludd, the latter related to the form of the famed Globe Theater. The theater, like any space, functions as a microcosm for the imagination.) Thus the art of memory served as both a mnemonic technique and a system of cosmic representation, a fact not lost on Medieval and Renaissance moralists: in such works as Cosmas Rossellius's *Thesaurus Artificiosae Memoriae* (1579), Heaven and Hell were both used as *loci,* as memory places, to constitude such mnemonic systems.[4] Utilizing these systems, we remember not only what we wish to recall, but also the larger ends of life according to the Christian ethos: the joys of Paradise and the torments of Hell, whose exigencies and finality guide all the endeavors of our lives. The very site of remembrance is thus transformed into a scenario of aesthetic moralization; the soul creates its own moral emblems with each and every act of remembrance.

When similitude rules as the method for remembering, we learn of the numerous modes of homology that may be established. Rossellius listed the following correlations: a *sample* (a quantity of iron to recall iron); *similarity* (the human being as microcosm for the macrocosm; ten fingers for the ten commandments); *metonymy* and *antonomasia* (Atlas for astronomy and astronomers; a bear for an angry man; a lion for pride; Cicero for rhetoric); *homonymy:* (the animal dog for the dog star); *irony* and *contrast* (the fool for the wise man); *vestigal traces* (the track for the wolf); *pronunciation* ("sanguine" for "sane"); *similarity of name* (Arista for Aristotle); *genus* and *species* (the leopard for the animal); *pagan symbol* (the eagle for Jove); *peoples* (the Parthians for arrows; the Phoenicians for the alphabet); *zodiacal signs* (the sign for the constellation); *relation between an organ and its function; common attribute* (the crow for Ethiopia); *hieroglyph* (the ant for prudence); and finally, *totally idiosyncratic association* (any monster of any sort for anything to be remembered).[5]

The last of these categories, monsters, is of particular interest to us in the present study. We here find ourselves in the realm of pure idiosyncrasy, in the farthest reaches of the imagination, in the realm before the world took form. One book, Ambroise Paré's *Des monstres et prodiges* [1573], lists thirteen reasons for the birth of monsters:

> There are several things that cause monsters. The first is the glory of God. The second, his wrath. The third, too great a quantity of seed. The fourth, too little a quantity. The fifth, the imagination. The sixth, the narrowness or smallness of the womb. The seventh, the indecent posture of the mother, as when, being pregnant, she has sat too long with her legs crossed, or pressed against her womb. The eighth, through a fall, or blows struck against the womb of the mother, being with child. The ninth, through hereditary or accidental illnesses. The tenth, through rotten or corrupt seed. The eleventh, through mixture or mingling of seed. The twelfth, through the artifice of wicked spital beggars. The thirteenth, through Demons and Devils.[6]

As is the case with memory systems—and indeed with everything whatsoever predating the rise of scientific culture in the West—we find ourselves once again situated between God and the Devil, between Heaven and Hell.

Monsters reveal the madness of the imagination, the manifestation of alterity and difference in extremis. Though each individual monster is of a formal rarity, indeed uniqueness, monstrosity in general is ubiquitous: monsters symbolize the life of the instincts and the terrors of the soul, the regions beyond the thresholds of rationality and the unexplored territories of the globe. The forms of monsters, to the extent that they can even be categorized, are even more varied than their causes: *confusion of natural kingdoms* (animal, vegetable, mineral); *confusion of sexes; hybridization; substitution of elements; hypertrophy* or *hypotrophy; lack* or *excess; indetermination* or *multiplication;* et cetera.[7] In this carnival of forms, these catastrophes of the flesh, we discover that primeval horror of a world which is not cosmos but chaos, a threatening, fearful world of primal matter yet unformed and essentially uninhabitable.

It is evident that these distortions, deformations and metamorphoses create the strongest impressions in our memory. For this very reason Cicero, in *Ad Herennium* (circa 86-82 B.C.), explained that the most successful mnemonic devices will be those that utilize the most striking images:

> We ought, then to set up images of a kind that can adhere longest in memory. And we shall do so if we establish similitudes as striking as possible; if we set up images that are not many or vague but active; if we assign to them exceptional beauty or singular ugliness; if we ornament some of them, as with crowns or purple cloaks, so that the similitude may be more distinct to us; or if we somehow disfigure them, as by introducing one stained with blood or soiled with mud or smeared with red paint, so that its form is more striking . . .[8]

If we wish to consider disfigured objects, monsters, "stained with blood or soiled with mud or smeared with red paint," the history of Western art provides no examples more striking than the grotesque dolls of Michel Nedjar. Compare Nedjar's own statement: "It was terrible and at the same time extraordinary. I covered my dolls over with soil and blood and it was a very powerful thing—I thought I was going mad."[9]

At first impression, entering Nedjar's attic workshop is not unlike penetration into the Capuchin catacombs in Palermo. In a domain where a natural or even alchemical *putrefactio* seems to reign, we are confronted with a plethora of "dolls" whose forms range from small mummy like papier-mâché objects to grotesque animals, from devils' heads and eyeless, troubled masks to shrouded, deathly ragdolls. These creations—made from refuse, garbage, leftover materials—are most often stained, filthy, spotted with paint, tinted from immersion in vats of dye: monsters from the earth, or the underworld. The effect upon the viewer—or perhaps we should say participant, for these are things to be touched, however difficult such a gesture may be—of each individual doll is disquieting enough; but the effect of the entire scene of this workshop, this matrix of creation (the "crowd effect" being one of the origins of monstrosity), is practically unbearable to those uninitiated in its mysteries. Nedjar's atelier might well be experienced as a sort of memory theater of the damned, and his dolls as doppelgangers of ourselves. Yet they resist us: their eyeless orbits blind them to us, and it is particularly disturbing that we are *not* seen by them, that they surround us in silent and blind proximity. And the effect of his own creations is reinforced by that of his collection of fetishes, talismans, amulets, gris-gris and magic dolls from around the world. [figure 7]

Nedjar suffered the usual interdiction against a boy playing with dolls. The repressed returned with a vengeance. These dolls are explained in Nedjar's own words:

> When I was a kid, my reality was a whole imaginary world in which I could live, in which I could live out my metamorphoses.
>
> When I was young, my parents wouldn't let me play with dolls because I was a boy, so I used to take a twig from a tree and wrap it around with cloth from my father's shop to make my own doll.
>
> I noticed that once I put a root onto a doll, the thing became a whole. Now I don't have to add on any roots, the thing already *is* a root.
>
> The body is a root. It doesn't emerge; the body lies underneath the earth. The root is nourished on earth. It lies underneath the earth.
>
> I used to get to the point where everything turned into a doll.
>
> When I make my dolls I feel like I *am* the doll that I'm making . . . [10]

The monster is often taken to be a premonitory sign, a divine warning (as the etymology of the word reveals). As such, Nedjar's workshop is a sort of *cloaca maxima* leading to Hell; the dolls are manifestations of unformed matter, matter resisting form, a certain decay of the spirit. They are sacred signs of the body represented not really before creation or after death, but rather in that ambiguous moment when creation is not quite complete, and death has not yet entirely finished its work. But what at first might be deemed imperfect is rather the very perfection of death's fecundity. The macabre is counterbalanced by fertility. Nedjar:

> Death is something—it's a birth, it's the continuity of things.
>
> In Mexico the mummies were so fascinating, it was too much. They weren't dead things at all. They still had their costumes on, their robes adhering to their skin.
>
> It's easier to slip down than to climb up. But falling—what creation within our existence—creation, exodus, hell, Auschwitz, Hiroshima, the plague, AIDS . . . " [Written on the back of a postcard of a Flemish painting, *The Fall of the Damned*.][11]

On the biographical level, Roger Cardinal was correct in inferring that these dolls served Nedjar as, "incoherent representations of the Holocaust, experienced as a kind of internalised trauma," for Nedjar's family suffered in the collective tragedy of the European Jews of that epoch.[12] These dolls are personifications of anguish, memento mori, simultaneously creations in order to remember and remembrances in order to forget; simultaneously a return of the repressed and an overloading of the memory system in order to forget; they permit that mourning without which history itself is an abomination, a lie.

In a fantasy that might be compared with Nedjar's own phantasms about dolls, Bruno Schulz, a Polish Jewish writer murdered by the Nazis in 1942, told the tale of his father, owner of a textile shop, who described a very different "cosmogony of cloth" when he declaimed a "Treatise on Tailors' Dummies, or The Second Book of Genesis." Speaking of the infinite fertility, inexhaustible vitality and seductive powers of matter, he explained that God has no monopoly over creation, and that we are all tempted to create. "There is no dead matter; lifelessness is only a disguise behind which hide unknown forms of life." Although God indeed possessed some important creative formulas, there are many others not yet attempted, which can be achieved even if by heretical or even criminal means. In a decidedly Nietzschean tone, he explained that, "We have lived for too long under the terror of the matchless perfection of the Demiurge," and we must thus escape this influence to release our own creative instincts.

> "We are not concerned," he said, "with long-winded creations, with long-term beings. Our creatures will not be heroes of romances in many volumes. Their roles will be short, concise; their

> characters—without a background. Sometimes, for one gesture, for one word alone, we shall make the effort to bring them to life. We openly admit: we shall not insist either on durability or solidity of workmanship; our creations will be temporary, to serve for a single occasion. If they be human beings, we shall give them, for example, only one profile, one hand, one leg, the one limb needed for their role. It would be pedantic to bother about the other, unnecessary, leg. Their backs can be made of canvas or simply whitewashed. We shall have this proud slogan as our aim: A different actor for every gesture. For each action, each word, we shall call to life a different human being. Such is our whim, and the world will be run according to our pleasure. The Demiurge was in love with consummate, superb, and complicated materials; we shall give priority to trash. We are simply entranced and enchanted by the cheapness, shabbiness, and inferiority of material."
>
> "Can you understand," asked my father, "the deep meaning of that weakness, that passion for colored tissue, for papier-mâché, for distemper, for oakum and sawdust? This is the proof of our love for matter as such, for its fluffiness or porposity, for its unique mystical consistency. Demiurge, that great master and artist, made matter invisible, made it disappear under the surface of life. We, on the contrary, love its creaking, its resistance, its clumsiness. We like to see behind each gesture, behind each move, its inertia, its heavy effort, its bearlike awkwardness.". . .
>
> "In one word," Father concluded, "we wish to create man a second time—in the shape and semblence of a tailor's dummy."[13]

These sentiments—in so many respects strikingly similar to those of Nedjar—are certainly a parable for artistic creativity in its modernist mode, where the materiality of the signifier is foregrounded, and where ancient forms are dismantled to construct an all-too-human scenario of the passions and mortality. For some, a perpetual state of the *non finito* is a necessary precondition for continued creation.

In contrast to an *ars memoriae,* Eco asked whether we can construct an *ars oblivionalis,* an art of forgetting. The answer is no: mnemotechnics as semiotics is strictly a means of making present, where every significative gesture entails a mental response. "If the arts of memory are semiotics, it is not possible to construct arts of forgetting on their model, because a semiotics is by definition a mechanism that presents something to the mind and therefore a mechanism for producing *intentional acts*."[14] There are no devices for forgetting per se, only for remembering or remembering poorly, "Thus, it is possible to forget on account not of defect but of excess . . . One forgets not by cancellation but by superimposition, not by producting absence but by multiplying presences."[15] We can force ourselves to forget by confusing the mind, by overloading it—occasionally to the point of madness.

Might this insight not serve as an interpretation of Nedjar's dolls? Might their creation not be an attempt to forget death by multiplying its instances and its icons? If, as Frances Yates has demonstrated, the cultivation of the arts of memory may have stimulated the creation of artistic and literary works—and if, conversely, certain poetic images have served as mnemonic devices—can it not be equally true that the desire to forget can achieve the same effects? This notion would provide us with yet a further refinement of that most ancient notion of the cathartic effect of art, where the past imposes itself on the work as *hysteresis,* as a belatedness of expression, as a rememorative recovery of origins.

The sixteenth century educational reformist Peter Ramus, in the spirit of a militant and iconoclastic Protestantism, devised a memory system that would do away with the iconic representations theretofore used in such artifice. He accomplished this by means of the famous "Ramist epitome," which absorbed memory into logic, whereby the subject to be remembered was arranged according to a dialectical order, a hierarchical classificatory system ordered to successively reveal the most general to the most specific characteristics of the subject.[16] Whether this system may be established as being a precursor to the Cartesian *mathesis universalis,* where the cognitive efficacy of iconography succumbs to the greater intuitive powers of axiomatic systematization, we might understand Ramus's memory system as an early attempt to rationalize the past and thus, by extension, formalize history, foreshadowing Hegel's crowning achievement in this domain. Everything is to be remembered, but as concept, not image. Rationality itself is internally structured as a cathartic mechanism.

Yet for some, catharsis is impossible, and new icons for the dead are still desired. In the year 1801, Pierre Giraud drew up a plan for a new type of cemetery, *Les Tombeaux ou essai sur les sépultures:* "In which the author recalls the customs of ancient peoples, mentions briefly those observed by the moderns, and describes procedures for dissolving flesh and calcining human bones and converting them into an indestructible substance with which to make portrait medallions of individuals."[17] In this project to ameliorate the horrendous conditions of the Parisian cemeteries, Giraud cited the work of a seventeenth century inventor, Becker, in whose *Physica subterranea* we find the notion of transforming mummies of fat into mummies of glass—what Dartigues would discuss as, "The Art of Vitrifying Bones." Thus, saved from the horrors of the tomb, the beloved would remain forever, in form and substance, by means of this new innovation in the cult of the dead. Philippe Ariès explained that this project confuses the language of two different periods and two distinct paradigms of treating the dead: "the period where the cadaver promised to reveal to anyone who dissected it the secrets of life and the period when the cadaver gave to anyone who contemplated it the illusion of a presence."[18] We might add that these two paradigms respectively reveal the contrasting modes of mnemonic systems that we have investigated: the logical and the iconic. Who is to say which is truly the most modern? Through which can we most effectively mediate the death of others, as well as our own, unrepresentable, death? How must we compare these medallions with Nedjar's creations? Mummies of flesh, mummies of cloth, mummies of glass: all are called upon, within a sort of necrology, to nurture memory, and all serve as signs of the memories that we are to become.

The attempt to form similitudes in the quest for remembrance leads to the most idiosyncratic imaginative variations; at the limits of these variations we discover, or create, monsters. Be they signs of the lineaments of our desires or the depths of our fears, it is nevertheless not only the sleep of reason, but also the rites of memory that produce monsters.[19] [figure 8]

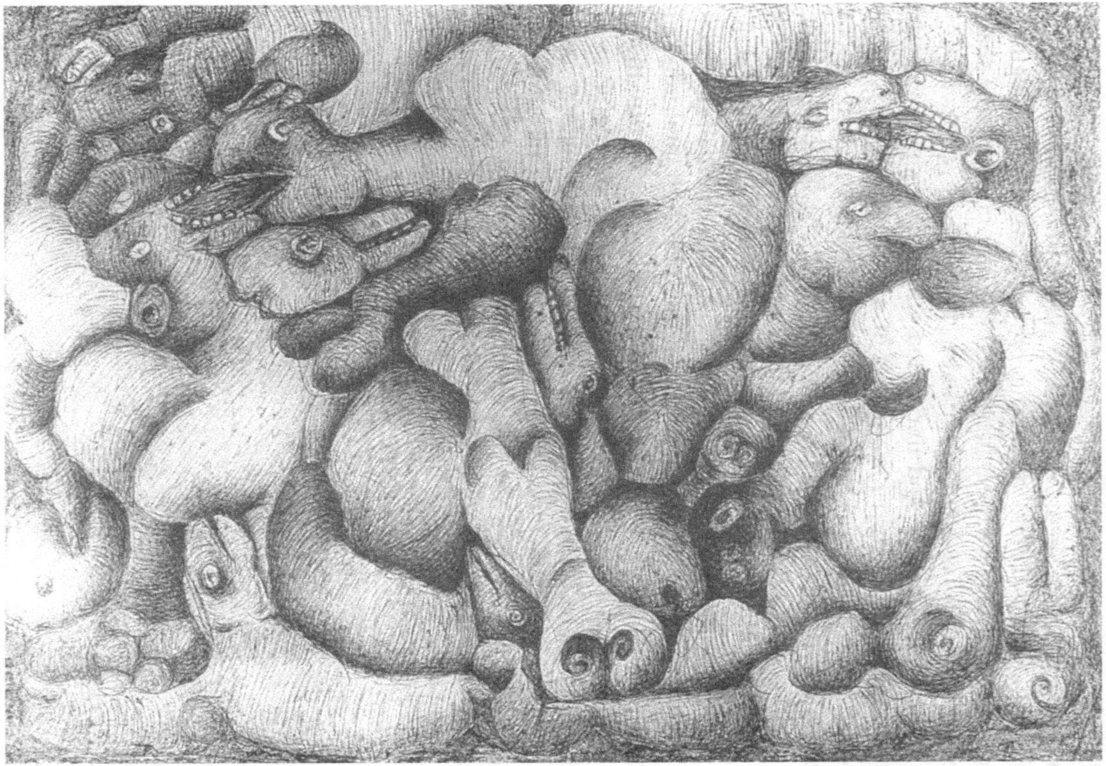

Figure 8. Vojislav Jakic, "Monsters," n.d. (photo courtesy the Collection de l'Art Brut, Lausnne).

THREE

Figurations and Disfigurations: On the Grotesque

> Only an image can please you *totally*, but never a human being. The origin of Angels.
>
> —*Elias Canetti*
> *The Human Province*

Mouths gaping in terror, or opened wide in awe, teeth clenched in fury; brows knitted in contemplation; eyes staring in amazement, closed in revery, teary with emotion; nostrils flared with passion. Except in sleep—when the world is interiorized, and desires are transformed into dreams—the human face is the seat of expression. Perpetually mobile, fugitive, tremulous, facial configurations are deemed a sign of the "passions of the soul," an indication of intentions, emotions, desires, thoughts. It is the belief in this separate but constant relation between interior and exterior worlds that gave rise to various theories of physiognomy, attempting to show that the very form of the human body—facial expressions, bumps on the head, lines on the palm, the placement of moles, and so on—revealed the form of the soul.[1] Yet these fields of study—physiognomy, phrenology, chiromancy (palmistry), metoposcopy, and so on—wished to describe a morphology of expression as if the body's static form were equivalent to the sum total of its active, gestural postures. These "sciences" attempted to transform the living, expressive body into an image, an icon, limited by the cognitive rubrics of interpretive systems. This reification of the face, purporting to explain its expressiveness, is precisely what denies all possible expression and individuation. Art and science are but the merest shadows of life.

The philosopher Emmanuel Levinas explained:

> Whereas a phenomenon is already, in whatever respect, an image, a captive manifestation of its plastic and mute form, the epiphany of a face is alive. Its life consists in undoing the form in which every *entity*, when it enters into immanance, that is, when it is exposed as a theme, is already dissimulated.
>
> The other who manifests himself in a face as it were breaks through his own plastic essence, like a being who opens the window on which its own visage was already taking form. His manifestation is a surplus over the inevitable paralysis of manifestation.[2]

Only in the representation of the human face, its conventionalized transformation into image, icon, sign, would facial expression and bodily gesture be deemed an adequate expression of the soul—except that artworks are objects and have no souls.[3] The soul cannot be adequately symbolized by external physiognomic features; it can be represented only by our acts. In a sense, there can be an adequate aesthetic symbolization of the soul only where there is no soul. The *expressions* of the living face may be considered to be *symptoms* of the soul's passions, in a mode of individuation; conversely, *representations* of the face must be understood as *symbols,* as a means of typification, and ultimately of stereotyping.

Consider, for example, the works of Oswald Tschirtner (of Gugging, the artist's house of a psychiatric hospital outside of Vienna), where the reduction of the human figure to a fully schematic form reduces all possibility of alterity. Here, all representations of the human form, including those of the radically different designations "I" and "You," are identical, because everything falls into the purest of formalisms.[4] [figures 9a and 9b] In these works a reductionist mannerism reigns: the body is typified within but one of its postural schemas, and our universe is reduced to a single formal element. Or else note the drawings of Rosemarie Koczÿ, where an obsessive repetition, organized by variations of the cursive gesture, reveals the limits of the human form in the mode of a gestural or postural anxiety. In the works of Tschirtner, the body is typified within but one of its postural schemas; in Koczÿ, the body is deformed to reveal the sum total and the limits of all possible corporeal forms and postures; while for Philipp Schöpke

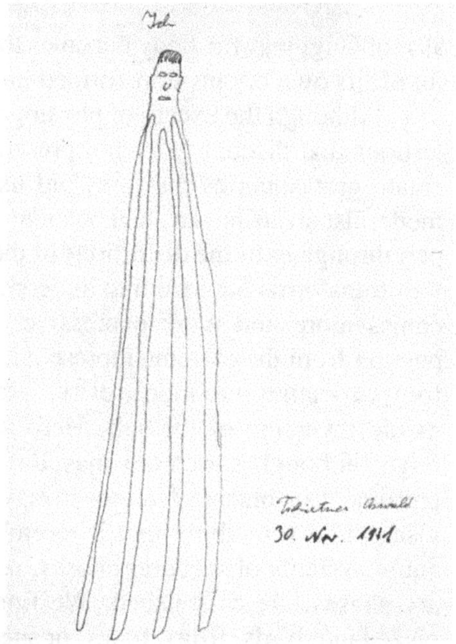

Figure 9a. Oswald Tschirtner, "I," 1971 (photo courtesy the Collection de l'Art Brut, Lausanne).

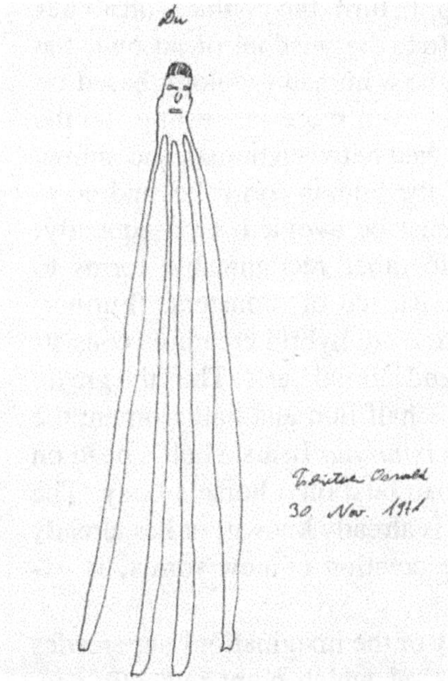

Figure 9b. Oswald Tschirtner, "You," 1971 (photo courtesy of the Collection de l'Art Brut, Lausanne).

also of Gugging, the body becomes transparent, inside and outside confused, its own organs transformed into foreign objects. [figure 10]

Although the excess of physiognomic schematization leads to distortions that disqualify such representations as science, it does in fact create grotesqueries that may aid us in understanding art; especially modernist art, tribal art, and outsider art—all of which function in great part through extreme distortions of the human face and figure. The portrait transforms the face into an icon, a symbol. Yet as the symbol becomes more and more expressive, the portrait loses verisimilitude, passing from the extreme representation of passion into caricature, and from caricature into monstrosity, into the totally other, revealing a demonic inversion of the self. Here we find that rules of resemblance reign: although caricature may distort the figure by aggrandizing a prominent or bizzare feature, it may also deform by transforming the visage into something that it resembles, most often an animal. Thus entire systems of metamorphoses, revealing a multitude of intermediary phases, are established. We find, for example, people metamorphized into birds, frogs, foxes, or sheep. In turn, the mythical attributes of these animals—the craftiness of a fox, the wisdom of an owl, the shyness of sheep—are used to determine a human typology based on corresponding types and attributes. But even more interesting, on the aesthetic level, is the continuity established between human and animal forms: it is as if radical distortions of the human form, beyond commonplace zoomorphic possibilities, must be avoided. Consequently, these deformations are channeled into other recognizable forms to elude visual chaos and eschew the existence of monsters. (Furthermore, we should note that most monsters are hybrid creatures consisting of diverse combinations of human and animal parts. Thus the *griffin* is half eagle and half lion; the *sphinx* is half lion and half woman; the *mermaid* half woman and half fish; the *minotaur* bears a bull's head on a human body, and the *centaur* a human bust on a horse's body. The imagination is usually limited by what is already known, or has already been seen; total monstrosity, and the creation of new forms, is extremely rare.[5])

Occasionally, the sheer "plasticity of the imagination" supercedes the restrictions of cultural acquisitions, at which point radically new forms are invented. This is most often the case in Art Brut, where by definition the isolated creative act shuns cultural determinations, finding sources of inspiration in other than acquired art historical forms.

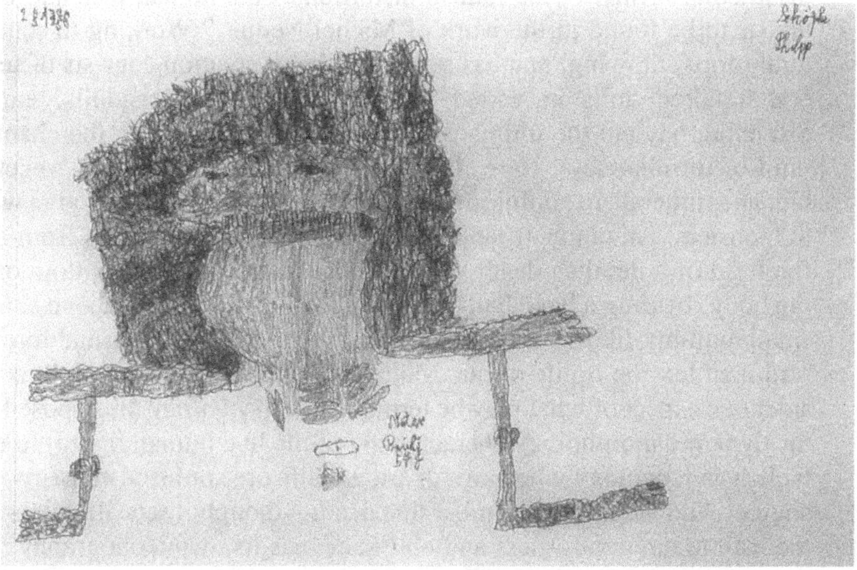

Figure 10. Philipp Schöpke, untitled, 1983 (photo courtesy Sam Farber).

One of the most extreme examples of such a production of new and disquieting forms, of the radical distortion of the human face and figure, is to be found in the work of Michel Nedjar.[6] Working in sculptural forms, drawing, and bas relief, his major creation consists of several hundred dolls in varied media (paper-mâché, ragdolls, etc.), extending beyond the ultimate bounds of the grotesque to the chaotic limit of formlessness. Here, the cosmic categories of animal, vegetable, and mineral are confused; hybrids are created; caricatures give way to monsters. An unidentifiable animal head with horns grows from the forehead of a devilish death's head; roots sprout from the bottom of a rag body, bearing a head half-way in decomposition from face to skull; small mummy-like objects are distended to give shape to primal forms; bird-men tax the limits of our zoological taxonomies. We might consider one aspect of what may be termed an *amorphology* (as opposed to the dynamic morphology characteristic of the live human figure) to establish an iconology where myth, art, and life are confused at their very source. And we must remember that death—though it sets all things on the path to amorphousness and oblivion—has its own iconography, its own play of forms, just as life does.

Both madness and possession trance were long believed to be manifestations of divine inspiration. Those voices heard in one's head, auditory hallucinations common to accounts of both schizophrenic patients and tribal shamans, may be deemed either a sign of the gods or a hypostatization of the soul, projected in a theological, paranoid, or aesthetic delirium. Because the head is experienced as the seat of human sensibility, it is also that part of the body which is most prone to imaginary attack by minuscule men, devils, scorpions, and other vicious animals, as well as that area prone to develop excrescences such as horns, other heads, or even foreign creatures. [see figure 5]

The anthropologist Claude Lévi-Strauss described an example of this in *The Way of the Masks*. Among a dozen groups of American Northwest coast Indians of the Salish linguistic family, one of the invariant features of their ritual *swaihwé* masks is that they sprout horns in the form of birds and often have a bird in the place of the nose. Lévi-Strauss explained that this symbolizes the relationship between heaven and earth, between contrary cosmological elements, marking the cosmic and mundane poles within which humanity finds its place.[7] Yet here, the symbolism is part of a fully developed sacred system; it signifies not a transgression of boundaries, but rather the articulation between the human and the divine, identifying the well-ordered axis between heaven and earth. The bird, a symbol of transcendence and a messenger of the gods, is also a symbol of the soul (of both the living and the dead) that connects our lives with those of our departed ancestors.

In mythical thought, the human domain is established in contradistinction to, and in continuity with, the realms of the animals and the gods. Humanity stands at the theological crossroad between the chthonic and the celestial, and the stability of the symbolic order is guaranteed by a series of prohibitions and ritual exigencies.[8] The order of the universe depends on a reign of purity, where all the elements retain their proper relations and homogeneity and are not mixed. Such a mixture leads to impurity and threatens a return to chaos. Thus, for example, the biblical dietary codes of the Old Testament demand that only the exsanguine flesh of animals be consumed by humans; blood is reserved for sacred sacrifice. The transgression of such prohibitions leads to disquietude, ontological instability, and even sin or tragedy. In a general sense, orthodoxy keeps everything in its proper symbolic place; heterodoxy is the result of an inmixing, which—from the traditional perspective—creates abominations. Precisely such abominations, such monstrous forms, provide one point of direct contact between human-beast and human-divine. The transgression of these proscriptive limits gives rise to pictorial expressions of the most radical metamorphoses, to prodigious creations of new forms.

Yet when we find such transformations and hybrid forms outside of a fully developed mythical or theological system—as in the works of Nedjar, where some humans take transcendental flight by being transformed into birds and others discover their earthly place by sprouting roots instead of feet or by slow metamorphosis into the devil—we must establish other contexts for their interpretation.[9] Yet all are not so lucky to have merely birds sprout from their heads as a sign of divine intervention. Daniel Paul Schreber, the "psychotic" whose *Memoirs of My Nervous Illness* was the text on which Freud based his theory of psychosis, in addition to the birds whose divine messages he heard sung to him, believed, that he was constantly plagued by scorpions gnawing at his skull, and three-millimeter men torturing his head.[10] We must consider the significance of the face—and the manner in which it may be troubled, distorted, effaced—to fully understand the impact of works of contemporary Art Brut.

If we were to establish a catalogue of facial parts represented in extremis, we would need to begin with the eyes, those "windows of the soul." The metaphysics of vision has been central to Western metaphysics since its origin in ancient Greece; the eyes, and the reciprocal play of gazes, have been a key compositional feature in Western representational art; the gaze is a crucial consideration of Freudian metapsychology. Why then, in so many works of Outsider Art, do we find eyeless figures? However, this accentuation of eyelessness does not necessarily signify blindness. This is particularly pronounced in the work of Nedjar, nearly all of whose dolls bear enucleated sockets, transforming these dolls and masks into death's masks. Why is this so? Is it somehow because, as Georges Bataille insisted, the eye is a "cannibal delicacy?"[11] Is it to hide the soul? (Do dolls have a soul to hide? Their absent souls are, paradoxically, symbolized by the very features that hide them. *Anima absconditus.*) Is it to instill fear in the viewer, thus serving as a sort of apotropaic charm to protect the dolls' maker and to guard his privacy? Is it the nostalgic manifestation of some childhood rite? We might remember that André Breton informed us that Nadja adores her little daughter because she resembles other little children, "with their mania for taking out their dolls' eyes to see what's there behind them."[12] Thus the absence of eyes reveals the *nothingness* behind the mask, as the empty sockets of a death's head reveals the void that awaits us after death. Fear, dissimulation, stigmatization, magic, metamorphosis, death: these dolls are antinarcissistic works, shattering the imago of the self beyond recognition, beyond merely human existence. Here, the extreme malleability of the image reveals the plasticity of the imagination, where gestural schema and physiognomic forms shed their humanness and disclose the primal forces of Eros and Death. The symbolization of death may be effected by protective narcissistic projections of flight and effacement, as well as by the contrary means of a fascinating, incantatory presence. In a sense, all masks are death masks: by transfixing the gesture, by stilling the dynamic formations and deformations of the living face, masks dissimulate the person while creating a *persona*. Nedjar's dolls are too varied to be totems or fetish objects. They are expressions beyond all possible narcissistic identifications and even beyond all possible narcissistic wounds. They can be considered to be our doubles only to the extent that, as the psychoanalyst Guy Rosolato explained, "The double, in effect, is not only similitude and replication, but also inversion, reversal, the negative."[13]

Whether to efface human individuality as a prerequisite for imminent confrontation with the gods or merely to hide oneself before the gaze of others, the mask transforms its bearer. Yet no mask is just a simple entity, offering a univocal identity hidden in its unique form. Lévi-Strauss explained:

> It would be misleading to imagine, therefore, as so many ethnologists and art historians still do today, that a mask and, more generally, a sculpture or a painting may be interpreted each for itself, according to what it represents or to the aesthetic or ritual use for which it is destined. We have seen that, on the contrary, a mask does not exist in isolation; it supposes other real or potential masks always by its side, masks that might have been chosen in its stead and substituted for it. In discussing a particular problem, I hope to have shown that a mask is not primarily what it represents but what it transforms, that is to say, what it chooses *not* to represent. Like a myth, a mask denies as much as it affirms. It is not made solely of what it says or thinks it is saying, but of what it excludes.[14]

Precisely for this reason the dolls and masks of an artist such as Michel Nedjar and the drawings of Koczÿ or Tschirtner must be viewed in a group of works. Not to recognize the individual mutations and abnormalities inherent in such figurations, but rather to stress the metamorphoses undertaken in the series as a whole. Only in this diacritical manner may the significance of any individual figure be recognized. This is more than merely a semiological argument: the experience of these works in quantity, seen in Nedjar's Paris atelier, cannot fail to shock and amaze by their cumulative effect. Only then will the apparently random distortions of the human form—sometimes verging on the purely unformed, revealing a chaos far beyond human possibililty—begin to take on meaning.

What is the threshold of this chaos? What are the limits of figuration? Where does iconophilia end and iconoclasm begin? In this regard, an emblematic oeuvre would be that of the man named simply "Max," a resident of the artists' house at Gugging.[15] Max has created a series of drawings consisting of elementary, and possibly elemental, pictures of people, which are then scribbled over.[16] [figure 11] We find here both an image and its own effacement presented simultaneously, indications of both the iconophilic and the iconoclastic impulses concurrently at work. In these drawings, approaching the aesthetic zero-degree of scribbling, we discover the limits of aesthetic possibility, limits shared with the dolls of Michel Nedjar.[17] Here, form and the unformed compete on equal terms for our attention; here cosmos and chaos mix, in undecided proportions. Can there be a more satisfactory answer to our questions about the soul, a more sufficient response to our disquietude?

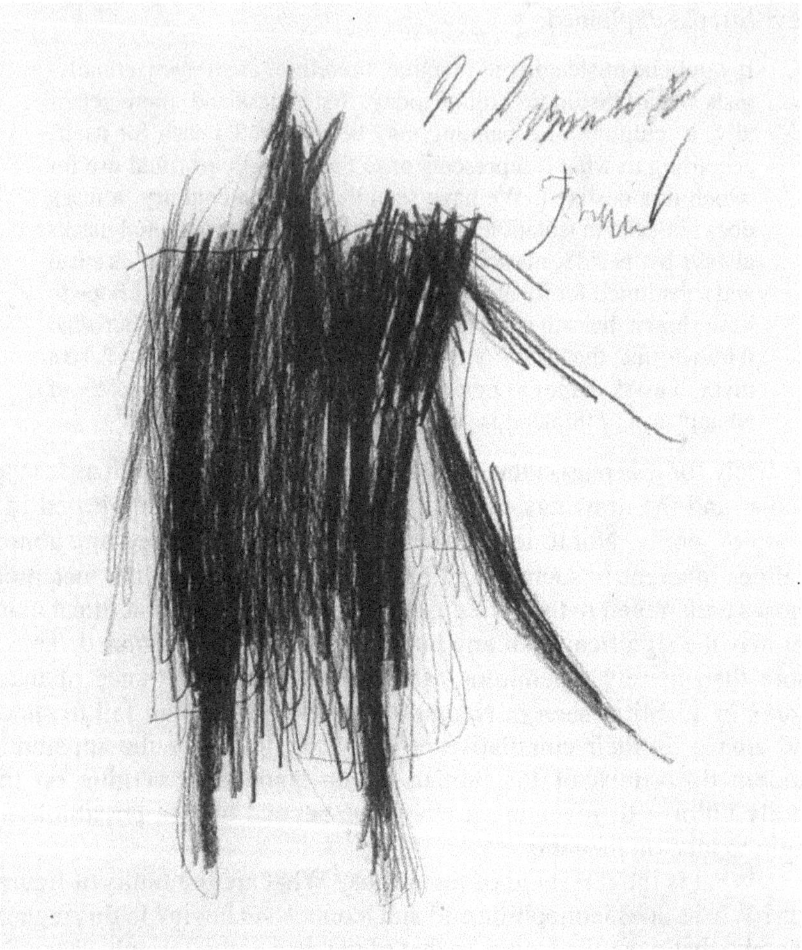

Figure 11. "Max," "Woman," n.d. (photo courtesy the Collection de l'Art Brut, Lausanne).

FOUR

The New Disfiguration

In a metaphysical vein, Gilles Deleuze suggested that modern art began when humanity "no longer saw itself altogether as an essence, but rather as an accident."[1] We might eliminate the Aristotelian paradigm and take this statement literally to ask: What are the aesthetic effects of the physical accidents that might beset the human figure? Nowhere has this been more evident than in the effects of war, through both its celebration (Italian Futurism) and denigration (Dada).[2] The aestheticization of war subsequently took on the conflicting forms of monumentalization, protest, catharsis. The tactical nature of trench warfare in World War I—that is, the need to look out from the trenches and the subsequent risk of having one's face blasted away—created a literal deformation, disfiguration, of the human form. This resulted in the creation of the prosthetic art of radical rhinoplasty (forerunner of cosmetic surgery), the literal recreation of destroyed faces. The formal exigencies of these wartime effects were not lost on the history of art; they should also be incorporated into the history of physiognomy. Whence the need for what Gregory Whitehead, in his radiophonic art, called the *Forensic Theater:* a semiology and libidinal economy of the fractured, fragmented, lost face.[3]

Emblematic of this aesthetic tendency is the career of Sacha Sosno.[4] Having provisionally given up painting after having seen the work of Yves Klein, he became a war correspondent for a decade, and in 1969 wrote the book, *Biafra, Proximité de la mort, Continuité de la vie,* a photodocumentary. His return to art coincided with the growing impossibility of gazing on such images, the need to efface these regions of suffering from his memory or at the very least to hide them from sight. His next works thus consisted of war photographs with the horrifying images blocked out by large rectangular areas of color—a sort of palimpsest of Yves Klein and Sacha Sosno, superimposing the aesthetic and the documentary. This constituted the origin of Sosno's art of *obliteration*. The transformation of this technique into sculpture consisted of the obliteration of classical models by means of either drilling a hole or passing a beam through the head, or wiping the slate completely clean by planing the face to a polished flat surface. These obliterations are a false iconoclasm: they reveal rather the dual iconophilia that desires to resuscitate classical sculpture *and* to preserve the flesh, being unable to suffer its destruction. This ethical dimension at the core of his work is based upon the paradox of needing to literally "deface" a work in which neoclassical casts have replaced classical originals and in which cold marble has been substituted for warm flesh. Yet the new work, by dint of its formalism, is so removed from the realm of the flesh, of the senses, that its origins—in the photos, in the war, in the mutilation of the body, in death—are forgotten. The work of sublimation is complete; stylization reigns.

So often, Modernist disfiguration of the female form, with its accompanying anguish, has been traced back to Picasso's *Demoiselles d'Avignon*.[5] But we are protected from this anxiety of mutilation by obligatory formalist devices: de Kooning's famed *Women* (1950–1953) receive their imprimatur by dint of their context within Abstract Expressionism, that most abstract of abstractions; Dubuffet's *Corps de dames* (1950–1951) lose their feminine specificity by being deemed metaphorical landscapes, aided by Dubuffet's own claim that these women (prefigured by his *Paysages grotesques*) must be understood not as particular forms, but rather as something immaterial, "on the level of a general concept." As both artists skirt the threshold of abstraction, the potential misogyny of disfiguration is transformed into an aesthetic celebration of figuration. It would seem, though, that we need only disengage ourselves from such art historical aestheticization to suffer the full psychological impact of these figures. Can the human form, being our own, ever truly be fully aestheticized? Can we ever really escape the psychological by recourse to the transcendental?

Francis Bacon's *Three Studies for Figures at the Base of a Crucifixion* (1944) was at least incidentally a wartime protest as powerful as *Guernica*. Bacon explained of the figures that, "I thought of them as the Eumenides, and at the time I saw the whole Crucifixion in which these would be there instead of the usual figures at the base of the cross."[6] As described by Robert Graves in *The Greek Myths* (I;31.g), the mythical

Eumenides, or Furies, "are crones, with snakes for hair, dogs' heads, coal-black bodies, bats' wings, and blood-shot eyes. In their hands they carry brass-studded scourges, and their victims die in torment. It is unwise to mention them by name in conversation; hence they are usually styled the Eumenides, which means 'The Kindly Ones'." The classical model creates monstrosity by classical means: the recombination of intrinsically frightening forms into a new whole. Bacon created an even more terrifying monster, by the reduction of animal forms to their primal state of torment.[7] His work may be considered in the tradition of Chardin and Soutine, where a fascination with animal viscera reveals, by extrapolation, the human body itself (and not the modern artwork) as the "anxious object" par excellence. Mannerisms of pain, the corruption of the flesh, the tortures of the body—this is precisely what Deleuze spoke of in regard to Bacon's work as, "a realism of deformation, opposed to the idealism of transformation."[8] Here, flesh is transformed into meat, life borders on death. Bacon: "I've always been very moved by pictures about slaughterhouses and meat, and to me they belong very much to the whole thing of the Crucifixion."[9] This is nowhere more evident in his work than in *Painting* (1946), where we see the dark dictator (his sharp-toothed mouth open, the eyes and top part of his head hidden by a black umbrella) set in front of a suspended carcass of meat, and surrounded by viscera—a sign of his deathly works, as well as of the evil form of his soul. Yet what disturbs us in these representations of meat is not simply the presence of dead animal flesh; rather, we are troubled by their function as signs of the animal nature of humanity, of the continual suffering of the living, marks of the spasmodic response of the body to pain. His further transformation of the human form—accomplished through a sponging or wiping technique that smears the paint, thus creating a region of indistinctness—takes the human figure just to the point of abstraction (the ultimate distortion, the final deformation) but never beyond. Now, the paint is tortured—Bacon, ultimately, is a painterly artist, and even his true fascination with the human form as potential slaughterhouse meat is always expressed, in his discourse, in terms of painterly effects, not historical events.

Michel Nedjar's grotesque dolls are, in part, a manifestation of the belated, internalized trauma precipitated by his adolescent discovery of the Holocaust. They are monstrous memento mori created as personifications of anguish.[10] His recent drawings, finger-painted silhouettes of men with nearly all detail eliminated, are both formally and psychologically a pictorial continuation and transformation of his earlier dolls. [figure 12] The earth tones, raw forms, tactile sensibility and distorted figuration are all still evident. In response to a question about his treatment of human physiognomy, Nedjar simply responded: "The human face fills in the void."[11] For Sosno, conversely, the void obliterates, or fills in, the face. Nedjar's technique maximizes the presence of bodily traces in the work; Sosno's eliminates them. Whereas the dolls responded to a cathartic need to assimilate death, suffering, mutilation and monstrosity through their very representation, the silhouette drawings efface all representations of those corporeal details that could proffer the signs of pain. A body without organs, closed to pain and history? The reversal of a primary desublimation? Or further sublimations of sublimation?

Perhaps some of the power of such works stems from the ritual origins of art—origins being rediscovered today, when our postmodern condition has sensitized us to the pre- and postaesthetic functions of art (especially sacred and ritual works) in both the Third and First Worlds.

> The votive significance of anatomical models in rituals of healing is generally known and accepted, and it has been suggested here that the deliberate mutilation of some Roman statues may be connected with this practice. The ultimate fate of works of art is in fact no less interesting than their origin or the purpose for which they are commissioned and used.[12]

Such iconoclasm is not, therefore, a function of religious hostility, but rather an apotropaic protection against such rancor. Here, iconoclasm is in the service of iconophilia; artistic representations of bodily mutilation are used to protect the fleshly body. We are reminded of a curious fifteenth century custom in the Rhineland: crucifixes were mutilated by soldiers to make their bodies invulnerable, so that, for example, to immunize their heads, they would cut the head off a crucifix. Yet this iconoclastic moment was often counterbalanced by an iconophilic one, for the decapitated head would be carried around as a good-luck charm. Might not the presence of certain artworks serve us as well? [figure 13]

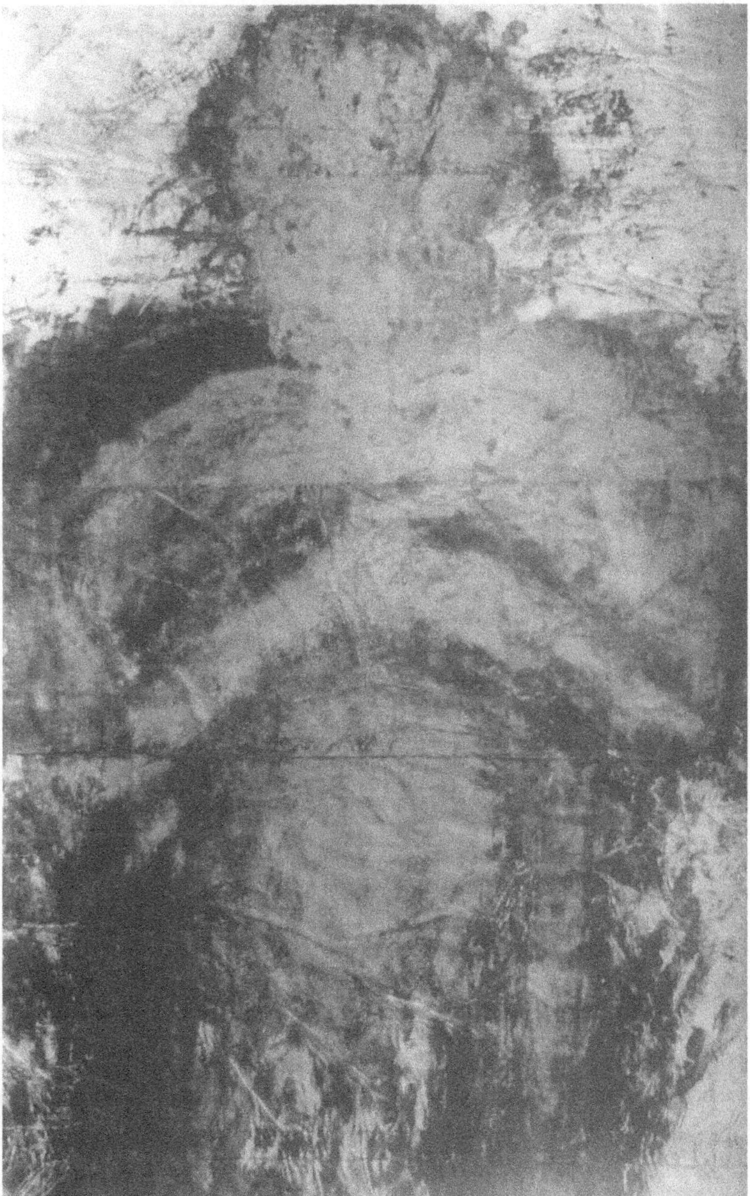

Figure 12. Michel Nedjar, untitled, 1990 (photo courtesy the artist).

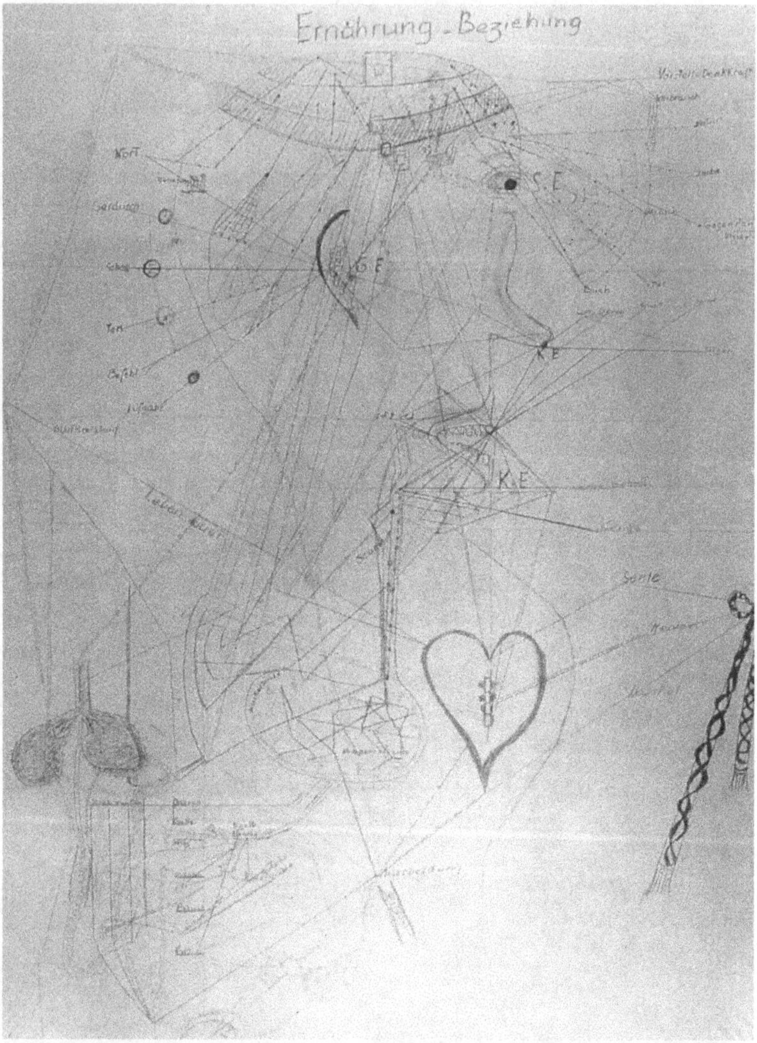

Figure 13. "Katherina," "Nutrition=Relation," n.d. (photo courtesy the Collection de l'Art Brut, Lausanne).

FIVE

Outside In: On the Problem of Demarginalization

Instead of thinking to resolve,
no longer think at all;
I am at the height of electrical magic,
I'm more and more there,
no longer to think, no longer to respond,
but to make magic,
not of enhancement,
but of horror,
theatrical,
and true.

—*Antonin Artaud*
Cahiers du Retour à Paris

In the Grande Halle de la Villette, on the site of the former slaughter-houses of Paris, now transformed into a cultural center, were exhibited two-thirds of the works of the exhibition *Les Magiciens de la Terre*, organized by Jean-Hubert Martin, director of the Musée National d'Art Moderne at Beaubourg, which housed the other third of the exhibit.[1] At the far end of the exhibition hall, dominating the central axis of the major visual trajectory, was a work by Richard Long: a gigantic circle painted directly on the wall in mud, an unlikely but supreme amalgam of abstract expressionism, Arte Povera, and neoprimitivism. On the floor at the foot of this work was to be found an Australian aboriginal sand painting created by six artists of the Yuendumu community. The juxtaposition is striking and not accidental. It is almost as if the painted body (depicted in the catalogue) of the ritualist celebrant who created this work in sand, and whose corporeal presence was in fact an integral part of the work, was absented to make way for Long's gigantic sphere, which now serves as the de facto symbolic focal point of the displaced aboriginal work. The living presence of ritualist creativity is replaced by the static apparition of another work. This juxtaposition and transposition may serve as an allegory for the entire enterprise of *Les Magiciens de la Terre*.

It has been suggested that the model according to which this exhibition might be understood is that of the "cabinet of curiosities," such that no overriding or overbearing logic determines the presentation of the selected works.[2] And yet we are well aware that every cabinet of curiosities has a history, bears a significance, and determines an art historical future.[3] Indeed, every possible grouping entails a totalization and creates a logic, if not a narrative. Whence the radical impossibility of escaping formalization within the museum context: not only is the museum a historical entity, but it also generates a parallel history, "art history," as if the latter were a world apart. The didacticism of the museum is but a stereotyping: without the supplement of the catalogue, the basically wordless space of an exhibition provides a context, imposes parallels and juxtapositions, and endows value. It is, by dint of its physical exigencies, primarily a place of recontextualization and appropriation, not of critique or understanding. And to further complicate the matter, in this epoch of postmodern discourse, every recontextualization potentially hovers between the hermeneutic poles of didactic critique and mocking irony, adding one more factor of indecidability to our experience of the museum exhibition. The museum remains the site of universalization via representation and the determination of values: spiritual, intellectual, economic, and otherwise. (Indeed, an insidious tactic of cultural appropriation is to give what is most free and most subversive the highest value in order to neutralize its practical efficacy.)

Perhaps nowhere is this presence of radical recontextualization more evident than in the exhibition of ritual objects from both the Third Worlds *(sic)* and from within our own culture. Much contemporary Third World art is highly politicized and critical, engaging the very relations that obtain between our different cultures—as works by Rasheed Araeen, Cildo Meireles, and Chéri Samba in this exhibition make evident. Yet sacred ritual objects tend to be more hermetically enclosed within their own symbolic systems: needy of initiation into their meaning, less engaged in external cultural communication, and thus more easily appropriated because less concerned with intercultural communication, commerce, and critique. They are, on the symbolic level, both recalcitrant and fragile. Within our museums these works become orphans, deterritorialized, wrenched from their own symbolic system. Yet the place that they find within our symbolic systems is superficial, guided by formal similarities, "affinities," by our own phantasms; in any case, their magic disappears in the daylight of our rationality. Our model of detached aesthetic contemplation belies the original complex situatedness of these foreign ritual objects whose efficacy is dependent on profound, and most often exclusionary, initiatory systems. We discover here precisely the theoretical point of articulation between not so much different "Worlds," but rather different symbolic systems. As postmordernist criticism insists, the critical point is the hinge between local and univeral, or at least universalizing, systems. Already, the notions of an "antiaesthetic" or an "anti-Oedipus"—radical, contentious, and destabilizing as they may be—are but local systems of thought within our larger, but still local, system of ecumenical pretentions.

It is precisely the initiatory aspect, a *knowledge* and a *practice* and a *passion,* of such rites and objects that necessarily escape us. We might remember, as a cautionary tale, the story told by Eric Michaels about the aboriginal television program where all the "we" saw was the most banal sort of "home video" depicting an empty, bleak landscape; but the tribal members observed the confluence of Dreamtime and historical representation, of myth and legend, in a landscape signifying an originary event of their culture.[4] It is precisely within such an ironic intercultural misunderstanding that the "magic of the earth" truly escapes us: even if we know of their history, and their gods, we also know that their deities cannot touch us. We can never truly know their art if we do not believe in their gods.

In *The Interpretation of Dreams,* Freud described an unreachable, uninterpretable, originary nexus of significations in the dreamwork; in regard to aboriginal art, Eric Michaels described the hidden knots of the symbolic that are culture-context dependent and pragmatically protected from the "outside," from "us," by the exigencies of their kinship and initiatory systems. It would seem that in all such cases (a fortiori true for traditional tribal communities) the ungraspable profundity of the symbolic is a function of pure contingency, of local, historicized situatedness. This nexus is precisely the point where the symbolic enters into history, where the particularization and the communalization of the individual are accomplished as contemporaneous events. Though there is always a signifier at this unattainable point, this signifier can be *anything* whatsoever—yet it remains unknown. Not because it is repressed, but because it is ineluctably real. Might this condition of symbolic organization be the precondition of faith—and of magic? Might we not discover here the formal efficacy of the symbolism of the earth, in all its polyvalent splendor and terror?[5] It would seem, in fact, that it is at precisely this point that structuralist anthropology finds its limit—at that point where the organizational pivot of the symbolic is no longer a *floating signifier* (which depends on the general, diacritical organization of the cultural system for its function) but rather a *lost signifier* (which is fully localized).

For example, the work at La Villette by Enrique Gomez, a Panamanian Cuna Indian, consists of a recorded shamanistic chant and its accompanying pictograms, the function of which is to cure madness. But the madness is not our own: as the social conditions that give rise to madness are culture specific, so is its treatment.[6] For us, this becomes just another artwork, another text, another ethnographic document. Quite to the contrary, Nancy Spero's *Codex Artaud* grappled directly with the problems of magic and madness at the very center of our own culture. By appropriating the work of Artaud, who himself was intimately concerned with the articulation of magic (Christian Mysticism, Kabbalah, the rites of the Tarahumaras Indians) and madness (which he incessantly suffered), she successfully worked through her own relation to the symbolic and derived from it a highly personalized and feminist art. And she accomplished this within a discourse and an iconology that is our own, even if situated at the margins of our sensibility.

But in *Les Magiciens de la Terre*, it is precisely the disjointed transcultural contexts that fascinate us, due to the paucity of contextualized description and interpretation. Whether we consider the works of the Third Worlds or of our own culture that are displayed in this show, what we regard are cultural displacements, not exchanges or transformations. As an example of what might constitute such an exchange or transformation, let us consider an example of our own, a work not represented in the exhibition, but rather discovered by chance just a few hundred meters away, in the flea market of Clignancourt (where, half a century earlier, the Surrealists did their own prospecting for found objects).

Michel Nedjar is a creator and collector of dolls of avowed magical powers. His habitation is thus a condensed focal point where numerous, and presumedly incompatible, types of magic meet, accumulate, and coalesce—finally to be transmitted to his own work. One doll in this collection, found in the flea market, is particularly striking and distressing: a classic Barbie doll, nude, blindfolded, thoroughly bound with black thread, and pierced with dozens of pins. [figure 14] We need but consider the tragic phantasmatic trajectory of this object to discover the complexities of intercultural symbolic exchange: from standard mass consumer toy to (most probably) urban voodoo object to collected artifact. This history in turn inspired Nedjar (and what other word can we use here but *inspired?*)—whose own biography enlightens us about a particular, even if arcane, destiny of dolls and dollmaking—who created dolls that in turn retrospectively endowed the Barbie with new meaning. The transformations and transpositions of this anxiety-producing (yet not particularly "anxious") object describe an itinerary that, if closely analyzed, might provide a detailed model of what *Les Magiciens de la Terre* might have been, had not certain constraints or stereotypes of the museum interceded.

The different lives of this doll remind us of the incommensurable differences between the domains of the personal-local-global (or universal): at each of these levels any given object takes on a different meaning, and any one of these levels can become paradigmatic of the others, yet none is pure or isolated. As such, the hermeneutic positioning of an object in a given level of the symbolic establishes the empirical conditions of an existential a priori; that is, of an axis or focus according to which all else is understood or interpreted. It is precisely here that a confusion of tongues, or a conflict of interpretations, may arise; it is here where may occur what Homi Bhabha writes of as, "a process of ambivalence in the structure of identification, which intervenes precisely in the elliptical 'between' where the other's shadow falls on us, and vice versa."[7] Whence the difficulties of the museum, whose paradigms remain modernist in a postmordern age—the postmodern pretentions of *Les Magiciens de la Terre* notwithstanding.

Postmodernism is not, except in its extreme banalization, simply an open-ended juxtaposition of objects or styles. (That would be but a

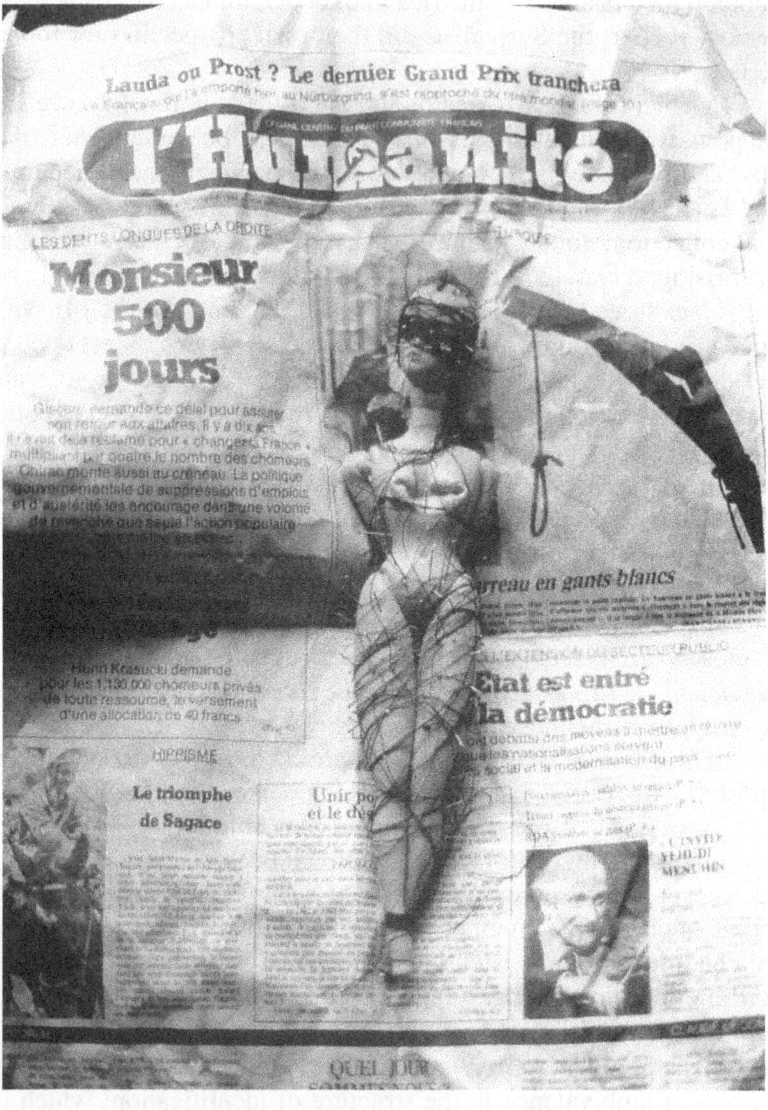

Figure 14. Barbie doll (photo Pascal Martin).

mere neo-Surrealism.) It is rather a juxtaposition of, and interchange between, cultures. Postmodernism is thus not a stylistic category, but a hermeneutic and sociological one, entailed by an infinite exchange and antogonism of information—concretely paralleled and "underwritten" by the infinite international flow of capital. Both information and capital constitute combinatory systems of change, exchange, and flow: there is no more outside; there are no more "outsiders." "Universalization" has finally been obtained; not through rationalized metaphysics, but through international capital. No pocket of resistance, once discovered, can escape—for how can one escape either sense or value? Let us by cynical about this and pose a parallel. Despite the radical, revolutionary rhetoric and intentions behind the "events" of May 1968 in France, this episode resulted in a reaction that only paved the way for the inroad of international capital. The peasantry, among the last bastions of traditional structures—then deemed reactionary—was destroyed; the working class bourgeoisified; and a disenfranchised underclass created. Might we not find a disturbing parallel in the "radical" theoretical discourse of postmodernism, which proposed the abolition of marginalization and which thus, despite the rhetoric of cultural specificity and local historicity, played into the hands of a rationalized-commercialized process now on the international level. Postmodernist aesthetics inaugurated the cognitive preconditions for the appropriation and commercialization of all that is marginal, be it within or without our culture.

This universalization and inflation of values has its linguistic counterpart, which is perhaps at the core of the problem that plagues *Les Magiciens de la Terre*. Quite simply, the words *magician* and *earth* here seem to encompass anything and everything, according to the curators' whims. (A precise explanation of the motivations for including each of the given works would be revelatory and perhaps disclose a cohesion and a curatorial logic that otherwise escapes us, despite the avowed curatorial desire precisely to avoid such a cohesiveness.) Through this linguistic inflation or vagueness, this lexical hyperbole, works by artists included in this exhibition such as Cragg, Haacke, Kawara, Paik, Wodiczko, regardless of these works' other values, are implied to be somehow "magical." This situation is epitomized and allegorized in Barbara Kruger's contribution, which is the first piece seen on entry to the exhibition at Beaubourg. This work consists of a large panel on which we read the question: "Who are the magicians of the earth?" followed by a list of possible answers: "Doctors? Politicians? Plumbers? Writers? Arms Merchants? Farmers? Movie Stars? Accountants? Artists? Secretaries? Soldiers? Tribal Chieftans? Beauticians? Priests? Computer Programmers? Journalists? Nuclear Physicists? Drug Dealers? T.V. Personalities? Mothers? Homeless People? Mathematicians? Nurses? Taxi Drivers? Linguists? Spies? Nuns? Lawyers?" Without attempting to discern the inner logic of this list, it becomes clear that the vagueness (practically anyone and everyone seems to quality as "magician") and the uncertainty (revealed by the sole use of the interrogative mode) expresses the very problem of this exhibition and perhaps the very difficulty inherent in our attempts to represent foreign and alternative cultures. Only by means of the trickiest figures of rhetoric can such a diversity of occupations (in the case of Kruger) and objects (in the case of J.-H. Martin) have been assimilated to the category of magic, especially in this context where works are displayed from other cultures where magic has a truly living context. Why not, then, choose from what is truly magical in the advanced industrialized nations (urban voodoo, religious mysticism, fetish objects) and not simply create yet more museum space for our already established artists? We meet here the curator as master rhetorician, or trickster. (For why should the latter category by uniquely relegated to African tribal or American Indian mythology?)

To conclude our remarks on *Les Magiciens de la Terre,* we might consider an exemplary, emblematic work displayed there, Jean-Michel Alberola's "Presque aussi facile de pisser avec des gants de BOXE (2ème partie), 1989," which is a found object, a ready-made, consisting of an eighteenth century Burgundian wooden bottlerack with accompanying documentation of purchase. The art historical reference is precise: Duchamp's ready-made "Bottlerack" (1914); the ironies are manifest: this object is a preindustrial formal precedent to Duchamp's work; the former in wood, the latter in metal; the latter purchased by Duchamp at Le Bazaar de l'Hôtel de Ville (a Paris department store), the former purportedly bought by Alberola in La Galerie Pierre Robin (a Paris art gallery specializing in primitive art); the first postmodernist, the latter modernist. What we have here is not quite an anxiety of influence (this would be a Borgesian mode of historicization), but rather an *anxiety of interpretation*. The object in question (Alberola's), rather than being anxious, is quite certain. Not a magical object, but a critical one, revealing a new rift at the center of our own artistic culture; not a juxtaposition, but an intercalation, reminding us of the once radical intervention of a work now become a masterpiece of modernism. Perhaps we could have been touched by the magic of the earth if we had achieved or witnessed the same sort of intercalation from within those other cultures represented here.

SIX

A New Anxiety of Influence

No artist has been more concerned, indeed obsessed, with the pure state of matter and the earth—as well as their aesthetic and antiaesthetic transformations—than Jean Dubuffet. His corpus is a celebration of the earth in the plethora of its manifestations. We need but consider the titles of several of his major series: *Sols et Terrains, Pâtes battues, Célébration du sol, Texturologies, Topographies*. The investigation of the materiality of the signifier, a procedure at the core of modernist aesthetic production, attained its hyperbolic statement in Dubuffet's project.

In *Dubuffet*, Michel Thévoz, curator of La Collection de l'Art Brut, which was formed by Dubuffet himself, provided a detailed study of this radical engagement with base materiality.[1] As understood by Thévoz, pure matter is opposed to the delimiting, identificatory exigencies of the form. Dubuffet's is an anticultural, antiinstitutional, antiaesthetic project. Yet this art, which aimed at a detotalization, destabilization, and ultimate disintegration of the cultural field, yet which ironically produced acknowledged masterpieces of postwar art, is indeed fascinating and instructive on the "formal" level.

Thévoz explained, in relation to Dubuffet's series entitled *Marionettes de la ville et de la campagne* (1942–1945), how Dubuffet manipulated "stereotypical elements anarchically in order to see what this morphogenetic disorder can produce in the field of representation" (p. 27). This process is true, mutatis mutandis, for all of Dubuffet's art: although the works themselves may approach the state of the unformed and engender a novel ugliness, their relation to the cultural field entails a new consideration of the very notions of formalism, representation, and beauty itself. His painterly methods provide a catalogue of inhabitual—indeed provocative, even inflammatory—techniques and materials, where the primacy of gestural traces is always at odds with an equal or even superior primacy of the intransigent stuff of the world. It is precisely in the aporia between gesture and material that the rationalizing process of thought and habit are circumvented, such that, for example in the *Texturologies* series, there is a conflation of pictorial signifier and objective signified (p. 123). As such, these traces and forms, "are not constitutively devoted to mimetic representation; they rather open the symbolic register up to its antefigurative polyvalence" (p. 36).

Thus Dubuffet is the artist truly inspired by matter, the "zero-degree" signifier, itself. As an art that preceeds "from jubilation and not from initiation" (p. 13), it would be a sort of creation if not *ex nihilo,* at least *ex materia*. "Let us say that this inspiration was found in his intimate relations with matter, with the earth, with carbonic or even radioactive gas, rather than in the paintings of Van Gogh or Picasso" (p. 20). The instauration of this mode of inspiration, presumedly beyond all cultural influence, was contemporaneous with Dubuffet's discovery of Art Brut: "It was the creators of Art Brut, discovered in the 1940s, which incited him to never again accept any teachings, especially not those of the works of Art Brut" (p. 20). This anxiety of influence—denying any influence of Art Brut on Dubuffet's own art—would seem to be the result of a curiously restrained model of artistic influence, as well as an overly positivist paradigm of causality, inhabitual in Thévoz's work.[2] We might suggest, as a more productive model, a theory of influence aligned with what Maurice Merleau-Ponty wrote of as, "the occult trading of the metaphor—where what counts is no longer the manifest meaning of each word and of each image, but the lateral relations, the kinships that are implicated in their transfers and exchanges."[3] Or, to speak in terms of rhetorical structures and processes, the possible modes of influence—in their formal, and not psychological, dimension—are as varied as the different tropes and figures of speech. Curiously, though, Thévoz hedged his bets: although all mention of the possible influence of Art Brut (which Dubuffet collected) on the works of art that Dubuffet produced are exorcized from the main text of the book, there is a return of the repressed in the notes. For here, interspersed with illustrative quotations from Dubuffet's writings, are comparative illustrations (albeit in black and white, as opposed to the splendid color illustrations of Dubuffet's work in the body of the text) of works of Art Brut, revealing the very influences denied in the text. It is, we suspect, only when these two oeuvres are finally confronted that the "definitive" histories of both Dubuffet and Art Brut can be undertaken.

The exhibit at the Peggy Guggenheim Collection in Venice (Winter 1986–1987) curated by Fred Licht, *Jean Dubuffet & Art Brut,* purported to answer the question of this relationship. Yet we find, expectedly, that the ampersand in the title signifies an exclusive disjunction! For we are immediately told, in Thomas Messer's Foreword, that,

> The relationship implied in the title of this exhibition, Jean Dubuffet & Art Brut, needs a word of explanation. For while the remarkable body of work by untaught artists assembled here was originally collected and even named by Dubuffet, it obviously bears no resemblance to the high achievement of an artist who has been of determining importance for the entire postwar period.[4]

We need not quibble whether Dubuffet's influence was in fact greater than that of Art Brut and especially its subcategory, "psychiatric art" (the latter best known through Prinzhorn's monumental work, *Artistry of the Mentally Ill,* published in German in 1922), an influence that deeply touched such artists as Pechstein, Nolde, Kubin, Ernst, Dali, Bellmer, Klee, the members of the CoBrA group Jorn, Atlan, Appel, and Alechinsky, as well as Richard Lindner and Nancy Spero, among many others. The question is rather to discern the motivation for denying what would seem to be, as we have stressed earlier in our reading of Thévoz, a major influence on Dubuffet. Indeed, Thévoz's contribution to this catalogue reiterates his earlier position: "Whatever it was for Dubuffet, *Art Brut* was not a new source of inspiration, even more anti-academic than the models; rather, *Art Brut* strengthened his resolve to repudiate his heritage in favor of an art without antecedents. The only lesson he learned from *Art Brut* was to learn no lesson, not even from *Art Brut*" (p. 11). The strategy, to argue for Dubuffet's greatness (which I hardly contest) and his originality (which could hardly be as pure as it is made out to be), necessitates the disjunction between Dubuffet's work and Art Brut. Dubuffet could be one of the great postwar artists precisely by being dissociated from Art Brut. To accomplish this, the works of Art Brut are set in a unique realm practically outside the space and time. In his catalogue essay, "Beyond the Reach of Critics?" Fred Licht, speaking of Art Brut, claimed that, "The artists of this tradition do not draw on any tradition" (p. 28) and later that,

> artists such as Wölfli and Aloïse live outside communal time. There is as yet no practicable way of relating their work to each other or to the events, fears and hopes of the time in which they lived. All notions of style that we have formed since the beginning of art history and art criticism are thoroughly exploded by their expressive art. (p. 35).

But in fact, these artists do live in a communal time, perhaps the most highly regimented community of all, that of the psychiatric hospital. Were we to seriously examine the effects of that sort of environment on creativity, then perhaps we could indeed relate their works to both our art history and our criticism.[5] It is precisely the fear of this "explosion" that prevents some from doing so and that causes the projection of this fear to appear as a fault of theory and criticism. We need a historicization of such art, not another myth of primal purity or unapprochability. (And this purity, of course, would be precisely that which serves as a defense against the influence of these works on Dubuffet himself.) Furthermore, we are told—in one more tactic to isolate these works from us, to make them appear alien, radically "other"—that, "The creators of *Art Brut* do not ask to be understood nor do they beckon us to follow them on their explorations" (p. 28). This belief echoes the oft-repeated claim, which has its origins in Dubuffet and is taken up by Thévoz, that Art Brut is "conceived without any regard for the usual recipients of works of art, or indeed without any regard for any recipient at all."[6] And yet, what we learn from many major contemporary studies of the expressions of madness, especially in R. D. Laing's seminal work on schizophrenia, is that the moment of creativity in mental illness constitutes not only a movement out of the deepest abysses of the diseases, but also that it is an attempt at communication and self-definition. Art history will not integrate these works into its domain in part because of the disquieting nature of these works and their origins and in part because of the unwillingness to become truly interdisciplinary, especially in regard to depth psychology. Not so much because of academic rivalries, but rather—out of caution, or out of fear—because there are certain things that one simply does not want to see.[7]

The artistic corpus perhaps most influenced by the art of the insane is that of Arnulf Rainer. In his own words: "I overpaint to find peace and quiet. There is nothing else that I like. Ideologically, only madmen and insanity have ever suggested to me enlightenment and possibilities for personal development. Seeds of culture in the classic psychoses fascinate me more than contemporary artistic currents."[8] Given the nature of the work in question, this position is even more radical than it at first appears. Rainer's technique of "overpainting" (*Übermalung*)—covering images with successive layers of paint, until the initial image is almost entirely, or occasionally even entirely, hidden—as well as his "finger painting" and "foot painting" (which achieve the same slashing, crossing, smearing, covering effects) are at the limits of gestural pictorial expression. Here, where gesture and painterly signifier are practically equated (and where the signified is practically lost to all but the creator of the work) the results are akin to the countless drawings seen in psychiatric hospitals around the world—precisely those crudest of "works," those scribbles, that do not even interest the specialists in schizophrenic expression or the collectors of Art Brut. Rainer recuperates the bottom limit of expressivity, the true *arte povera,* to establish his own oeuvre.

Curiously, in the 1989 Guggenheim museum retrospective of Arnulf Rainer, no mention is made of such influences in the catalogue essays. In both the foreword by Diane Waldman and Rudi Fuch's essay "The Labyrinth," great care is taken to establish a standard art historical lineage or pedigree for Arnulf Rainer. His influences are indicated as being Dada, Surrealism, Expressionism, Tachism, Abstract Expressionism; Klimt, Schiele, Arp, Klein, and Mondrian; as well as children's drawings and even the traces of chimpanzees (the latter of which Rainer himself indicated as an interest). Yet all the while they neglect the facts that (1) Rainer reiterated his special interest in the art of the insane: "the only things that appealed to me were mental patients' drawings and the autistic theater of catatonics, an art form devoid of pseudosocial trimmings"[9]; (2) he possesses a renowned collection of psychiatric art (and is particularly familiar with the artists' house at the psychiatric hospital at Gugging in Austria); and (3) he has written publicly on the topic.[10]

We find in this museological procedure the confusion of value and meaning: although Art History can be the arbiter of *value* judgments, it can hardly determine the meaning of works once it suppresses the study of history, depth psychology, cultural studies, and so forth. And in this case, while resisting possible interpretations drawn from the exterior of its domain, it also resists evidence stemming from within Art History itself, that is, the very existence of Art Brut, one of the inner limits of our aesthetic experience. In doing so, the work of Arnulf Rainer is ostensibly demarginalized and transferred to the mainstream. But can this resolution resist Rainer's own "Lamentation" about certain finger paintings and foot paintings?

> Here I am sitting now in my studio, a physical wreck, faced with a mass of trivial, spoiled, bungled, scrawled to death pictures not knowing how to ever finish them, without once more going through that state of utter fatigue and destructive exhaustion.
>
> Can new evolution be expected to emerge out of defeat, fatigue and exhaustion? When considerations, comments, incriminations and self-humiliations make the whole pile of rubbish clear, gloom and despair seize me. How should I get rid of this load of corpses of paintings?
>
> How and where should I bury them? How and where should I burn them?[11]

This is the same question that so many directors of psychiatric hospital archives ask themselves when faced with endless piles of their patients' drawings, without ever having gone through the creative process or the trials of madness themselves. Rainer's response, whatever it may be, can never be their own, nor ours. And, if we are to begin to understand the import of this question, we must ask ourselves: What is the meaning, the import, of these "psychiatric" artworks to their creators? The answer will surely open a heterogeneous field of investigation, where the conventional critical problems and history of "art" will begin to pale.

These varied remarks reveal a twofold phenomenon at the core of certain tendencies in postmodern art criticism and curatorship: (1) the attempt at a total demarginalization of works previously excluded from the art historical canon; (2) a denial of the influence of these very same works on established mainstream artists. This new anxiety of influence is an attempt to maintain the myth of the "originality of the avant garde." Yet in fact what is accomplished is precisely the assimilation of a former avant garde into the mainstream, all the while sequestering certain influences, now demarginalized works, into a new rubric of art history. We can only hope that this will create some new margins and some new marginalia.

SEVEN

Art Therapy, Outreach, Art Brut

The limits of art and nonart, art and antiart, art and life are vague. If anything, twentieth century aesthetics has expanded the scope of art such that it is impossible to define, much less locate, its limits, its margins. Outsider Art, Art Brut, remains a marginal art; yet here too its own limits are blurry. Let us consider a margin of Outsider Art—not Neuve Invention, which tends toward mainstream art, but rather those myriad works produced in the context of hospital art workshops and art therapy created by social and psychiatric outreach groups. This will permit the simultaneous reopening of the question of both the limits of art and, more specifically, the limits of Outsider Art.

Such art workshops must be differentiated from Art Therapy. Art Therapy has therapy as its primary goal, and not the creation of art (though, it occasionally inaugurates true art); to the contrary, art workshops have the creation of "art"—even if at a rudimentary, didactic level—as its primary aim. Furthermore, such art workshops present a totally heterogeneous field of instruction: each artist who participates has his or her own pedagogical technique, ranging from total laissez-faire to detailed, directed instruction.

The argument, generally forwarded by those historians of Art Brut who follow Jean Dubuffet's antipsychiatric tendencies, most notably Michel Thévoz, is basically that the low quality of the works created in such conditions (whether in art therapy or outreach workshops) disqualifies them from being art. (John MacGregor, in *The Discovery of the Art of the Insane,* disqualified them without due justification, though not from an antipsychiatric viewpoint.)[1] Two comments are opposite here. We must first ask why there is the insistence that the history of Outsider Art must be constituted by a series of masterpieces.

Postmodernist theory has taught the dangers of such a limited paradigm for museological decisions. (Such a mode of aestheticization had systematically excluded from art history the art of women, racial minorities, and until recently tribal art—as well as the art of the mentally ill.) The question of museological criteria of selection leads to two distinct impasses in regard to Art Brut: (1) its limitations to a history of "masterpieces" that has plagued modern art; (2) the total lack of aesthetic criteria often seen in the collections of psychiatric hospitals nowadays. But what of second-rate art and third-rate "modern" art? A walk through the Soho galleries in New York should easily convince us of the existence of such minor works, exhibited as "art" alongside the acknowledged masterpieces. Contemporary sociologically oriented art history and criticism has demonstrated precisely why, for example, the history of photography must be supplemented by consideration of snapshots, the history of cinema complimented by the study of home movies, and the history of video art revised by deliberations on the role of television. It would thus seem that the history of Outsider Art should follow this aesthetic paradigm and expand its purview to lesser works. Quite simply, not everything deemed art is great art. If we are willing to speak of mediocre and even poor works of art in general—as is the job of every art critic of differentiate—why are we not willing to do so for Outsider Art? Why this double standard? Why should Outsider Art be a category that contains only masterpieces? The borderline between aesthetics and sociology should remain vague.

Second of all, it should be noted that the art therapy situation itself has indeed motivated the creation of "masterpieces," rare as they may be. Consider Michel Thévoz's description of the origins of the art of Johann Hauser, considered by many to be the greatest contemporary creator of Outsider Art among those patients living in psychiatric institutions: "It was only in 1959 that he began to draw at the invitation of Dr. Leo Navratil. . . . From 1966, Dr. Navratil, for administrative reasons, was in a position to treat Johann Hauser in the following manner. A bond was established between them. This stimulated his drawing and he commented on it voluntarily. He became more and more communicative."[2] Clearly, Navratil recognized something special occurring in this art therapy situation, something that needed to be pursued on *aesthetic* grounds. If this art therapy did not produce art per se, then at the very least it motivated the future creation of art. Nevertheless, this quotation is, of course, a precise description of art therapy. And, after all, is not the work of people like Drs. Leo Navratil and Johann Feilacher at Gugging precisely a form of outreach and art therapy? Granted, it is more subtle, more talented, and more inspired than most others. Is not their very presence and care certainly part of their therapeutic concerns, part of the "inspiration" of the Gugging artists? Dubuffet wished to say, with his usual radical polemical tone, that such cases are not those of madmen turned artists, but rather artists who become mentally ill. But in fact, it would be perfectly reasonable to claim that, in Hauser's case, his presence—for better or worse—in the psychiatric hospital milieu and the beginnings of his therapy provided one of the major motivations, and perhaps inspirations, of his work. (And, for the record, to cite the inverse case we might remember that those works of Jackson Pollock created in the context of his Jungian art therapy are also ultimately considered to be artworks, and the effects of these works on the development of his subsequent oeuvre should be noted.) But even such major exceptions aside, why should the condition of production of works in a therapeutic or workshop setting disqualify them a priori from being art? We cannot anticipate or second guess the sources of creativity. What may create blockage for some may be an inspiration for others.

Outsider Art is a heterogeneous field, composed not only of the art of the mentally ill, but also of the art of eccentrics, isolates, and so forth. The semantic construction of the term, proffers a twofold qualification of its objects, necessitating a double investigation of the field. As the term *art* qualifies a category of objects, Outsider artwork must be aesthetically judged and studied by means of all the devices of our critical, hermeneutic and art historical apparatus. Conversely, the term *outsider* qualifies not the object, but rather its maker and the conditions of the production of the work. It is thus a sociological and historical qualification, necessitating quite different interpretative disciplines. (In this sense, the term *Outsider Art* is more accurate than *Art Brut,* because, even though Dubuffet's notion of Art Brut is a mixed aesthetic and sociological qualification, the term *brut* seems to qualify a pictorial aspect of the works in question, many of which are not at all "brut" or crude.) Thus in each case we must decide whether a work is "art" (and this regardless of any "brut" quality, as, for example, sheer gestural psychopathological symptoms might be "brut," but are not art.) But once this aesthetic decision is made, we must then make the sociological decision as to whether that very same work is "Outsider." These relations are schematized here to clarify, not to simplify; needless to say, such decisions are made simultaneously within a comprehensive consideration of the cultural field. To the contrary, all arguments made according to a merely intuitive recognition of what constitutes Outsider Art lack the rigor of true aesthetic judgment. In each case the decision must be made on aesthetic *and* sociological grounds. We can never know by merely considering the work itself whether it is Outsider Art or not. To make aesthetic judgments on mere intuition is journalistic art criticism, not art history or theory.

Two major presuppositions exist at the core of such intuitively founded arguments: first, that the generalized post war use of medicalization in the psychiatric hospitals somehow destroys the creative faculties; second, that those works produced in art therapy and art workshop situations are highly directed and not created spontaneously, which thus mitigates against their aesthetic authenticity, against their originality. Might we not simply respond that it is precisely the influences of these patients' medicines, their doctors, and their art teachers that they must overcome to create art!? In any case, as already noted in regard to the question of originality and directedness in artwork, not all such outreach situations are directed. But more generally, the modernist myth of a pure originality in the arts must be overcome. It is art, or at least culture, that begets art; and the origins of the artwork are always elsewhere than in merely some primal "intuition" that mysteriously inspires the artist. In both premodernist and postmodernist discourse on the arts, it is recognized that artistic creativity takes place in constant dialogue with the tradition, a dialogue that contitutes a labyrinthine series of motivations and influences, both retrospective and projective. Curiously, MacGregor found himself on both sides of the argument. In *The Discovery of the Art of the Insane*, he began the invaluable work of showing the varied cultural influences at work in the creation of art by the mentally ill. And he especially pointed to the importance of such figures as Navratil in regard to their inspiring work with patients. Yet in his essay in *Portraits from the Outside*, perhaps because of his desire to maintain a rhetoric of originality in the arts, he parenthetically insisted that, "nothing that goes on in art schools *ever* results in producing an artist."[3] It is as if all modern art were reduced to the state of Art Brut; that is, to a presumed eschewal of influence. This hyperbolic claim, this anxiety of influence—mimicking the inflammatory rhetoric of Dubuffet—has little of Dubuffet's precision; for, even leaving aside the

Medieval guild systems and the Renaissance apprenticeship relationships, does MacGregor really believe that there was no value whatsoever in the entire histories of L'Ecole des Beaux Arts, the Bauhaus, Black Mountain College, the Slade Institute, or the Parsons School of Design and The New School for Social Research, to cite just a few examples? Art is not simply pure creativity: it is also learned technique—even in Art Brut, where technique may exist tacitly, but where it nevertheless exists. The advances in aesthetic theory in our postmodern epoch have, one might hope, done away with the modernist vestiges of the Romanticist notion of originality and individual genius as the ultimate determinant criteria of aesthetic value. Why has this anachronistic value system persisted in the field of Outsider Art, just at the very moment that it attempts to finally enter art history? As a counter example, consider Oswald Tschirtner's drawing of Christ, which is a copy of Holbein's dead Christ—and which was, like all his other drawings, instigated by Navratil. Shall it thus be disqualified as art because it is a sort of copy made at the behest of someone?

What is the cause of this anxiety of influence? Perhaps one answer is quantitative. Until now, the number of works and list of creators included under the rubric of Outsider Art were quite limited, originally consisting of Dubuffet's own collection (now the core of the Collection de l'Art Brut in Lausanne); and even now there is a relatively small number of collections to augment this vision. To the contrary, the works produced in art therapy and outreach workshops exist behind a vast floodgate, and consist of millions of pieces. (For example, the archives of the Museo do Inconsciente in Rio de Janeiro consists of well over 100,000 works done by patients in Jungian therapy. We should also note that the many patients of the psychiatric hospitals of Rio represented in this collection have not, for the most part, received either psychotropic drugs or art therapy. Contrary to Thévoz' arguments, these practices have not been universalized in the post-war years, as they are still greatly absent in Third-World countries.) To even begin to consider the scope of such works, much less to search them all out, would be an unmanageable task. This quantitative problem threatens the various hegemonies created by the exclusion of such works from the rubric of Outsider Art: it makes impossible the establishment of a comprehensive collection, a comprehensive exhibit, and even a comprehensive knowledge; thus threatening curator, collector, and historian alike. Furthermore, in regard to both collectors and gallerists, it shatters the present market dynamics, where Outsider Art (for better or worse) is a low-cost art whose prices are in the process of rising (and, in some cases, such as that of Wölfli, Ramirez, and Hauser, the prices are already equivalent to those of much contemporary art). To introduce into this restricted market a vast number of works and thus flood the market—even if, as is indeed the case, the great majority of these works are not even fractionally as interesting as the "masterpieces" in question—would quite possibly diminish the desirability and marketability of those rare works that have entered the Outsider Art "canon." Thus the desire to mark the end of the production of Outsider Art in psychiatric hospitals in terms of postwar medicalization is, in part, an attempt to stem this flood and thus to quantitatively, qualitatively and chronologically restrict the field and maintain a certain aesthetic "purity." A Romantic myth of creativity is used to establish the conditions of aesthetic and economic scarcity. The closure of the field is an intellectual *and* economic safeguard.

Or is this really so? Is this fear really justified? Perhaps, and just perhaps, such an opening up of the margins of Outsider Art would increase and generalize our interest and thus make the great works shine even brighter. In any case, it would certainly create a more adequate social and historical context for understanding the production of such alternative art. We should remember that Dubuffet's original notion of Art Brut was that it be the art of the common person, and thus an art that worked precisely against the notion of the masterpiece. And it is not the case, as John MacGregor mistakenly claimed in his catalogue text for the *Portraits from the Outside* show, that "Originally Art Brut was entirely synonymous with Art of the Insane."[4] It should also be remembered that Dubuffet would make a special point, while describing the contents of his collection, to explain that only about 50 percent of the works came from people institutionalized in psychiatric hospitals.[5] It is ironic that Dubuffet's polemic, which was intended to open our eyes to works we had never previously considered to be art, has now been transformed into a myth of origins that creates the domain of Outsider Art as one of exclusivity, rather than inclusivity. Dubuffet wanted to constitute a notion of art that worked against the idea of the masterpiece, and we find ourselves denying works entry into the domain of art because of a certain lack of aesthetic value. What is the basis of this judgment, other than the opinions of certain critics? Is this how Outsider Art is to enter art history? Art history must not be confused with art criticism. It would seem, as it always was for Dubuffet, that the critical and theoretical rhetoric of Art Brut should be one that forces us to look, and not one that incites us to disregard.

Here, Michel Thévoz was far more subtle, and more correct, than MacGregor. According to Thévoz, the curatorial museological procedures of Outsider Art constitute, in part, a theory of exceptions. Questioned for *Portraits from the Outside* about the relations between Art Brut and Neuve Invention, he responded following Dubuffet's distinction between Art Brut and the cultural arts; that is, by saying, "Art Brut and cultural art are poles between which are situated, on a continuous terrain, all sorts of more or less hybrid creations. It is precisely this more or less which defines Art Brut and cultural art."[6] Dubuffet ultimately realized that no work is entirely immune from cultural influences. Such categories must thus remain approximative, according to Thévoz. This transgression of boundaries—first apparent to Dubuffet in the work of Gaston Chaissac—is precisely the phenomenon which establishes the ever-fluctuating limits of Outsider Art. Furthermore, it is apparent that there are exceptions to the rule that no art has been produced in Western psychiatric hospitals following the rise of widespread medicalization: notably Carlo, whose work was, incidentally, created in an Italian psychiatric hospital art workshop, and the patients at Gugging. But it is precisely the flexibility and vagueness of these categories, and the willingness to make these exceptions, that permits continual aesthetic discovery. Every normative aesthetic is doomed to its own limitations.

The final argument against the inclusion of art therapy and outreach workshop works in the rubric of Outsider Art is a pragmatic one, heard over and over; that is, the retort that one has never seen such works of quality and originality, and that one would be willing to change opinion on the matter if ever such works could be found. Of course, this is a no-lose argument: once aesthetic matters are based on personal, and not historical and sociological, criteria, the critic, in the face of any given work, can merely disclaim its aesthetic value and return to point zero. Questions of quality hide issues of exclusion. In response, consider, for example, works in the New York based Hospital Audiences Inc. collection, or those of the Museo do Inconsciente. Just as Dubuffet and Thévoz created a margin of Art Brut called *Neuve*

Invention, one would only hope that another margin of Outsider Art based on such works of outreach groups and even art therapy, can be created, to recuperate certain inspired, and inspiring, artworks from the historical trashcan of psychiatric symptomatology—just as earlier manifestations of the art of the mentally ill, as well as all other sorts of Outsider Art, were saved thanks to the inspired work of Prinzhorn, Dubuffet, Cardinal, and Thévoz, among others.

But in conclusion, we might note one more danger, another sort of exclusion—this time not for economic, dogmatic, or ideological reasons, but rather out of sheer self-interest. One of the major difficulties in approaching such works and their creators is quite simply the emotional difficulties surrounding our relations to mental illness. To enter into psychiatric institutions in search of such works would expose us to the extremely painful visions of mental illness, to the difficult and often hopeless treatments of mental illness, and to the often disquieting living conditions within the psychiatric institutions. This is an experience radically different from—and infinitely more difficult than—seeing works of art on display in galleries or museums. The efforts of those people who perform this reaching out, and make such artwork possible and visible, must be highly commended—and even more so, they must be praised for bringing some joy and value to the lives of people whose existence has often been otherwise forgotten, suppressed, repressed.

Yet even here there are problems, related to the very nature of the organizational structure of these institutions. Very often, outreach groups (which, as in the case of Hospital Audiences, Inc., may create huge archives of the works produced by their patients; see their catalogue, *The HAI Collection of Outsider Art, 1980–1990*), receive their renewable funding from a variety of sources, often partially from public funding. It would seem that at times there is an insidious myth about mental health and psychiatric cures at work here. Might it not be the case that occasionally the administrators of such institutions believe that they must project a certain public image of their own social work; precisely to assure the continued funding of their operations? Might there not be an unfortunate commonplace prejudice at work here, whether actually believed by these administrators or merely cynically applied in the realpolitik of institutional existence, a belief that the display of disturbing, tormented, grotesque works might imply to some people the failure of such art therapy or outreach and the related belief that the creation of bright, "cheerful" works by these patients would imply their success? If this is the case, then the public manifestations of such institutions would serve as a sort of propaganda device, necessitating the selection of works to be displayed according to the perceived public-relation needs of the institution. The conditions of selection and exhibition are in part a function of the (certainly often misguided) perceptions about the difficulties and exigencies of public and private funding. An institution would not want to threaten its public image, and consequently its funding, by displaying what might be construed as signs of its own failure to cure. If, on the other hand, this policy of exclusion is effected with the welfare of the artists in mind, following the belief that the display of morbid or distorted works would entail the artists' stigmatization, then it must be said that such a belief belies an extremely naive view of both aesthetics and mental health.

Thus the prevalence in many such exhibitions of brightly colored, rather joyous works—with their banal, often childlike, rather unoffensive subject matter—might be accounted for by such censorship. There is also the more basic question of which works from the workshops are to be saved for the archives and which works abandoned or destroyed; which, from among those works saved, are to be made available to outside curators; and which are to be finally released for outside exhibition, reproduction, and study. (Needless to say, the huge volume of such works does not permit everything to be saved. Nor would it be desirable to preserve it all, given the admittedly repetitive, derivative, and stereotyped aspects of most of this work.) And yet, as long as scholarly access is prohibited, we cannot even begin to fathom the results or the quality of such works and thus cannot make the sorts of judgments against them here in question. An inaccessible archive is an affront against knowledge and community. Furthermore note that perhaps one of the motivations of a group such as HAI to prohibit the sale of the works of the patients in their workshops (even though these works, including those selected for the archives of HAI, officially "belong" to the patients) is in part a matter of attempting total control over precisely what is made available to the general public.[7] As many people who have worked with mentally ill patients in such workshops will attest, many of these patients do indeed wish to sell their works, and some certainly wish to be recognized as "artists"—a profession and self-recognition no better or worse than any other. Denying them this possibility, even despite their meager chances of success, is to kill a dream and condemn them to remaining "patients"—hardly an enviable limit to their self-definition.

But there are other, more profound and more direct, modes of censoring or "directing" works. Although it is true that the contemporary prevalence of drug therapy eliminates many of the extreme mental states that previously gave rise to dark, distorted, tormented works, it is also true that such works continue, to a lesser extent, to be produced. Only now they tend to be dissimulated. It is equally true that the choice of material given to these patients—for example, often pastels and watercolors instead of india ink or oils; standard drawing paper instead of crumpled newspapers; sparkling glitter instead of filthy rags; and so on; in short, "clean" instead of "dirty" materials—determines in great part the resultant "look" of the works produced under such circumstances. This too, in effect, is a sort of censorship—a censorship by standardization that we all suffer in our everyday lives due to the advances of a mechanistic, technocratic, computerized society.

We must beware of the search for an unmediated vision in a world where nothing is unmediated, where every object is part of a historical, cultural matrix of signs and values—as every major aesthetic theory from Phenomenology through Structuralism and Post-Structuralist Deconstruction, has taught us. Dubuffet's original polemic was intended to open our eyes, to create a field of fascination, and to expand the boundaries of art. We must avoid the danger of appropriating this polemic in very different historical times, to create an institution, to categorically demand exclusions, and to hold certain works hostage to the limitations of our theories. Rather than closing our eyes, we must discover new ways of seeing.

Part II.

Other Modernisms

EIGHT

Écrits Bruts: The Other Scene of Writing

The anchored mind,
screwed into me
by the psycho-
lubricious thrust of
the sky
is the one that thinks
every temptation,
every desire
every inhibition.

o dedi
a dada orzoura
o dou zoura
a dada skizi

o kaya
o kaya pontoura
o ponoura
a pena
poni

It is the penetralia of the spider-web,
the eithoric female hair
of either-or the veil,
the anal plate of anayou.[1]

So begins Antonin Artaud's *Artaud le Mômo* (1947), a text that exists at the intersection of the genres of poetry, autobiography, manifesto, protest pamphlet, and psychopathological symptom. What place does it have in modernist literature? Is it an example of what Michel Thévoz, following Dubuffet, termed *Écrits Bruts?* How are we to read its ostensibly nonsensical neologisms and glossolalia? How does it relate to his earlier theatrical work? Does this unique language evince a certain insufficiency, or rather a hyperreal grasp of the tortured depths of the psyche and the terrifying expanses of the cosmos?

The presumed insufficiencies of language have haunted writers throughout the ages. Indeed, at the basis of Nietzsche's critique of Western epistemology and morality is a linguistic diatribe against conceptuality. In "On Truth and Lie in an Extra-Moral Sense," he explained:

> Every concept originates through our equating what is unequal. No leaf ever wholly equals another, and the concept "leaf" is formed through an arbitrary abstraction from these individual differences, through forgetting the distinctions. . . . What then is truth? A mobile army of metaphors, metonyms, anthropomorphisms—in short, a sum of human relations, which have been enhanced, transposed, and embellished poetically and rhetorically, and which after long use seem firm, canonical, and obligatory to a people: truths are illusions about which one has forgotten that this is what they are . . .[2]

Jean Dubuffet, who in 1945 began his research into Art Brut, established the parallel notion of Écrits Bruts to account for those texts which do not fall under our standard cultural purview.[3] Here, the normative genres and narrative forms of literary and discursive writing are overturned; vocabulary is reinvented, syntax shattered, and orthography transformed. Dubuffet's rationale parallels that of Nietzsche:

> And yet we also have the feeling that the repertory of words utilized in each of our languages is extremely narrow in relation to the innumerable apprehensions of thought, and that each of these words suffers a great poverty in their abstract status, in order to translate the particular situations of each designated thing and the associations which link thought to it. It is said that there are fifteen different ways of saying "camel" in Arab, and there are without a doubt as many ways of saying "seal" or "snow" in Eskimo. But do only fifteen suffice? A hundred times a hundred thousand are

> needed. And in this regard, we still wouldn't have enough. For thought is in motion, while words are inert bodies. What we need is words in motion.[4]

Consider, for example, the writing of Gaston Duf, also known as Gaston the Zoologist, interned in a French psychiatric asylum in 1940, where he began to paint and write. Observe his transformations of the word *rhinocéros:*

> Rinâûçêrshôse
> Rhin'-Oçêrhâûshe
> Rin'-hâûçêr-hâûs'he
> Lin'-hôçêr'-hâûs
> Irâûçerâûse
> Rônâûsêrôse
> R'-inôçêrôse
> Rhin'-hhhâûçêrôs
> Rinôsâirâûs[5]

The issue of religious, mediumnistic, and psychopathological glossolalia (babble) is exemplary. The procedure of discovery and appropriation is twofold: while modernist procedures opened the possibilities of accepting nonclassical forms into art, aesthetically attuned psychoanalysts and linguists disclosed their own discoveries of such forms, making them available for transmogrification into the artistic realm. Glossolalia—which entails the enunciation of the pure signifier, the refusal of meaning, and the reduction of speech to the pure voice, of language to the body—manifests that foregrounding of the signifier that now seems to be a central tenet of modernism. In turn, the valorization of such forms in early modernist poetic experimentation—Italian Futurism's *Parole in libertà,* Russian Futurism's *zaum,* Tzara's dadaist experiments, Schwitter's *Merz,* Surrealist automatism, and later in *Lettrisme, Sound Poetry,* and so on,—all championed the interest of glossolalia as poetic devices. The shift in discursive formations permitted the incorporation of psychopathological symptomatology into aesthetic production, broadening the range of aesthetic possibility. In turn, these broader aesthetic criteria permitted the very productions of the insane to be deemed art, an aesthetic paradigm shift that ultimately permitted Dubuffet's researches into Art Brut and Écrits Bruts. A final stage of this process can be seen when the investigators themselves create works following such linguistic inventiveness, such as Henri Michaux's and Dubuffet's literary pieces or, more recently, the theater of Valère Novarina.[6]

The linguistic and psychological characteristics of Écrits Bruts may be considered in either psychopathological or aesthetic terms. As one example among many, Jean Bobon, in *Introduction historique à l'étude des néologismes et des glossolalies en psychopathologie,* provides a compendium of the varied linguistic effects of mental illness: neologisms, paralogisms, agrammatism, paragrammatism, glossolalia, glossomania, dysphasia, dyslogia, paraphasia, neologia, schizophasia, paragraphism, an so forth. Indeed, one might go so far as to presume a different linguistic disorder corresponding to each possible rhetorical trope and figure! Michel Thévoz, revealing his antipsychiatric sentiment, spoofs these categorizations:

> Mallarmé's writing is characterized by *atelophemia, idiophemia, leipophemia, paraphemia, stereophemia* and *apatelophrasia,* while that of Joyce manifests tendencies of *polyphemia, spasmophemia, tachyphemia, dramatophrasia, embolophrasia, cataphrasia, echophrasia, planophrasia* and *schizophrasia*. In fact, we see that in terms of neologisms and "jargonographia," the psychiatrists hardly lag behind their patients.[7]

Yet how must works of Écrits Bruts be treated? Do they indeed fall within the category of literature (modernist or otherwise)? Must they be relegated simply to the realm of psychiatric symptomatology, or is there a unique category within which they must be grasped? Consider the most famous example, that of Adolf Wölfli, whose case history is acknowledged both by Dr. Prinzhorn in *Artistry of the Mentally Ill* (Berlin, 1922), a book that greatly influenced the Surrealists, and by Dr. Morganthaler, who wrote a monograph on Wölfli in 1921, the first book to seriously treat the work of a psychotic as art. Wölfli, who was confined in a psychiatric asylum in Switzerland in 1895, began his artistic production of pictures and texts in 1899. His illness was characterized by weakened associations with the outside world, hallucinations, flights of morbid imagination, megalomania, religious deliria, extreme identifications, persecution complex, guilt, fixations, autism, memory disorders, affective disorders, linguistic disorders, depression, catatonic symptoms, dementia, violence—in short, nearly the entire gamut of psychopathological symptoms of schizophrenia. How much of this was due to his illness and how much to what would be a normal reaction to the severe conditions of his incarceration is impossible to ascertain. Wölfli's mode of nomination already indicates one of the origins of his creative mechanisms: associations between words and objects having broken down, the referential function exists in the tautological realm of the pure imagination. His discourse is a sort of solipsistic stream of consciousness, guided by pure obsession, to which we possess only a small part of the referential code. Here, the relations between words, as well as between fixations and obsessions, determine the flow of his writing. Sound, rhythm and rhyme, rather than referential meaning, rule the texts; formal, and not representational, aspects rule the images. Wölfli's linguistic disorders alternate between both limits of aphasia: the total breakdown of syntax into fragmented words *and* the total rule of syntax, such that words no longer have any representational meaning beyond their linguistic context. Both nonsense verse and senseless narrative abound. Thus we find, dispersed throughout his writings, glossolalic texts which may be considered either as tone poems or magic formulas:

> Mitta z'witt!
> Hung noi noi,
> Bitta Stritt!!

Are not these "disorders" indeed characteristic of certain stylistic features of modern poetry? Furthermore, the "descriptions" on the reverse of the drawings, which may be deemed a sort of modernist narrative, are as little indicative of their object as the narratives are descriptive of the real events of his life. Rather, they are perhaps affectively representative, as in the case of the text on the verso of the drawing *Chimberasso-Forest:*

> Explanation. The picture in front, (copperplate engraving,) is from north to south, 12,000,000, hours long, 8,000,000, hours wide, and 9,000,000, hours, calculation-rate or, 80,000,000,000,000, square-hour, surface-content-enclosing—Chimberasso-Forest, in North America. The Giant-City, Chimberass-Forest-Hall, from whose enormous center, St. Adolf-Giant-Monument, I fell fatally, in summer, 1,867, has, as circa, 5 times as large as Newyork, about: 1,000,000, hours, in calculation rate. Variattion No.. 4, on the picture, shows, how my then beloved, the holy Santta Roosa, Greatgreat-Goddess, passes her hand over the cheeck of my beloved Father, St.Jakob I., as a result of a previous, mutual quarrel,

> so that he was immediately, forced, to seek medical aid. Thus it happened at the Chimberasso-Forest, South-forest-Thunder-Wall, from which I fell fatally from the high alpine-ridge at the time.? Yes!! And that one. Sacred Thund'r, Orang Uttang-, Monkey, on that narrow stone-strip up there: That one, obviously, is still right now acting like a pig. Respectfully signs and greets, St.Adolf II., Bern, Switzerland. 1,918.[8]

Here, the sublime unites with the banal, the catastrophic with the monumental, the imaginary with the nonsensical. Rather than being true "explanations," these texts are a continuation of his voyage, a literary extension of his pictorial quest, which all create a disturbing aesthetic interference with our standard modes of everyday expression.

The most famous "litarary" case in point would be Daniel Paul Schreber's *Memoirs of My Nervous Illness,* the text on which Freud based his theory of psychosis. Schreber's paranoid, psychotic "drama" began in 1894, when he was commited to a psychiatric asylum. He believed that he was to be "unmanned" (castrated) by God so as to be divinely fecundated and create a new race of men to restore the world to a lost state of bliss; his delirium included the belief that his existence was controlled by divine miracles, and yet he was constantly tormented by sexual abuses, by a cacophony of voices, by "soul murder." He feared that the world was to end in catastrophe, and he was to redeem it.[9] In the year 1900, at the very moment that Freud's *The Interpretation of Dreams* was published, Schreber (who had read Kraeplin's work on psychosis), after having surmounted his initial bout of madness, wrote his memoirs, which he presented as proof of his mental competency to regain his civil rights and control of his estate. Are these memoirs literature? In "Writing and Madness," Octave Mannoni argues that the writings of the mad constitute a unique literary genre. Yet even within this genre, we must at least distinguish between those works written during the period of madness and those other, albeit rare ones, written in retrospect, after the illness has passed (as is Schreber's case). The latter sort tends toward an often theological narrative account, whereas the former tends toward the fragmentation of the linguistic system. The difference between the original mad event and its retrospective account is that, as Mannoni explained, in the former,

> What gets lost is whatever agency may be capable of critiquing the originally given hallucination . . . of constituting it elsewhere in fantasy, where it can freely be without being. This would amount

> to freeing itself as pure speech and making us both the fool who can say anything and the king for whom the words of his fool are of no "consequence."[10]

What is at stake here is to establish precisely how the "other scene" of the unconscious, of a certain imaginary, of madness, is discursively constituted, and how the subject is constructed and situated within this linguistic apparatus. Mannoni suggested that, "asylums, like the one where Schreber was kept, are like 'prosthetic' substitutes for this other place, when it is lacking, in that asylums materially and actually isolate what cannot be denied."[11]

But this is already to speak from the psychiatric-psychoanalytic viewpoint. Jean Dubuffet forcefully protested against such distinctions (although not, in the following citation, quite pushing his argument to its antipsychiatric conclusion):

> Besides, this distinction between normal and abnormal seems quite untenable: who, after all, is normal? Where is he, your normal man? Show him to us! Can the artistic act, with the extreme tension that it implies and the high fever that accompanies it, ever be deemed normal? After all, mental "illnesses" are extremely diverse—there are almost as many types of mental illness as there are mentally ill people—and it seems quite arbitrary to throw them all into the one special basket of "illness." From our point of view, the artistic function is identical in all cases, and there is no more an art of the insane than there is an art of dyspeptics or of those with knee problems.[12]

This position is seconded by Dr. Ferdière, who was castigated by Artaud as being his torturer, but, it must be added, under whose care at Rodez Artaud began to write once again in 1945, after almost eight years of alternating between (often raving) madness and aphasic silence, during which time he produced few works. Ferdière:

> There is no more a psychopathological art than there is an art of "morbid consciousness"; in a general manner, one barrier after another falls, barriers which, even yesterday, separated the normal from the abnormal; madness now truly takes on a "human value." Psychiatry must have no other goal than to "found a general phenomenology of the imagination."[13]

In itself, we cannot distinguish a "sane" from an "insane" idea or work. Any notion such as Art Brut, Écrits Bruts, psychopathological art, *les fous littéraires,* and so on, is simultaneously an aesthetic *and* a sociological determination. The pathological or brut aspect of such works can be determined only by sociological-psychological considerations; that is, in terms of the material conditions of their creation. Insofar as we are concerned with the influence of such works on modern art, we need consider only their formal effects, but we should remember that these works contributed not merely new forms, but also new sensibilities, to modernism. These forms must never be dissociated from their accompanying sensibilities: thought exists within the flesh. Artaud: "There are intellectual screams, screams that come from the *delicateness* of the marrow. That is what I call the Flesh. I don't separate my thought from my life. With each vibration of my tongue I retrace all the paths of my thought within my flesh."[14] For the depths of mental illness reveal the extreme possibilities of the human condition: horrendous psychic pain, radical isolation, total depersonalization, fragmented perceptions, distorted concepts, obsessive activities, theological catastrophes, and mystical bliss of the highest order. Does this reveal an anticultural position or does it rather disclose the true depths, the dark, suppressed face, of our existence?

In either case, Antonin Artaud's anticultural works of his last period, that which began in 1945 in the asylum at Rodez and continued until his death in 1948, are as eloquent, authoritative, and potent as those of Dubuffet. In 1968 Dubuffet wrote a short book entitled *Asphyxiating Culture,* a timely resumption of his lifelong battle against what he termed, in a derogatory sense, the *cultural arts*. Artaud, in an early work, "Fragments of a Diary From Hell" (1926), wrote of his own psychic state: "I don't need food as much as a sort of elementary consciousness. This knot of life where thought emissions hang. A knot of central asphyxiation." The difference is that although Dubuffet's antagonistic rhetoric was created at the height of lucidity, Artaud's arose from the irrational psychic turmoil of his suffering and, eventually, his madness. Artaud's is an exemplary case, being both a great writer and a *"fou sublime."* His theatrical work remains among the most influential of the century; his "mad" writings remain, for the most part, unread. Indeed, his case is unique: excluded from Dubuffet's *Art Brut,* excluded from Breton's *Anthologie de l'humour noir,* excluded from Thévoz's *Écrits Bruts,* excluded from Blavier's *Les fous littéraires,* excluded from John Oakes' *In the Realms of the Unreal,* Artaud presented one of the rare cases where great writing and eloquent madness converge. An investigation of the discursive and cultural conditions that made this conjunction possible will expand our understanding of both Artaud and the boundaries of the literary manifestations of Art Brut—Écrits Bruts.

NINE

Music and Madness

In his first book, *Le Schizo et les langues,* Louis Wolfson, who describes himself variably as, "the student of schizophrenic languages," "the mentally ill student," "the student of insane idioms," provided a "mad" linguistic theory to explain his particular relation to his mother tongue, English.[1] The book consists of biographical fragments interspersed by, indeed interrupted by, phonetic analyses of his new use of language. Wolfson, who wrote this book directly in French at the age of 39, while living in New York City with his mother, was an obsessive, paranoid schizophrenic, who had suffered several incarcerations in psychiatric hospitals. Not being able to bear his mother's voice, and by extension, the sound of his "mother tongue," Wolfson utilized several strategies for escaping from this painful idiom: plugging his ears with his fingers (which left little possibility for other activity); plugging one ear with a finger and the other with a radio earplug (which did not alleviate matters); wearing double radio earplugs and later Walkman headphones (which at least freed his hands). These varied "deafeners" functioned by either blocking out sound or replacing the hated sounds of the English language with either foreign language programs or music. Thus, in a sense, his entire life was lived to a constant background music.

But all of these were passive defenses; his masterstroke was the active, spontaneous, immediate transformation of the English language into a sort of panglossic double. He accomplished this by means of his study of several languages, most notably French, German, Russian, and Hebrew. Three methods were employed:

1. He could achieve this transformation word by word, by means of finding a homophonic synonym in another language, such as the German *Milch* or the Danish *mælk* for the English *milk* (p. 41).

2. For more complicated terms, he could disarticulate the word and provide several syllabic substitutions, culled from different languages; for example, in regard to the term *vegetable shortening, vegetable* is easily transformed into the French *végétal,* but *shortening* poses more difficulties. The first syllable /sh/ needs to be broken up into the Hebrew *chemenn* (grease) and the German *Schmalz* (grease); the syllable /or/ is transformed into the Russian *jir;* and suffix *ing* becomes the German *ung* (pp. 54–55).
3. Or he would invent neologisms, for example the substitution of *urlich* for *early* (p. 127).

Thus, to escape the torments of a living language, Wolfson retired to the dead language of dictionaries, letting lexical coincidences rule his discourse. Yet here is the paradox, and the irony, of his situation: his linguistic method is circular, because the homophonic substitutions ultimately only transform the hated English into something sounding like English—but with a totally idiosyncratic, very heavy, polyglot accent! He traversed the languages of the world in order to return to the suppressed English idiom, just as his perpetual attempts to escape from his mother's voice would eventually lead him to reflect on his ultimate bond to it, and to her. Indeed, at the very end of this book, he claimed that he hoped some day to be able to speak English normally once again.

Yet the very possibility of such linguistic studies was effected by the passive defense mechanism of listening to music on the radio, which drowned out his mother's voice. And we should note that music also played a role in his mother's vocal "attacks" on him. She used to love to sing, one of her favorite tunes being "Good Night Ladies," and at one point began to accompany herself on a portable organ. It was music against music. His use of language was not communication, but a move toward psychic isolation; similarly, his appreciation of music was not in terms of pleasure or expression, but rather a self-isolating defensive mechanism. Perhaps the most poignant exception to this isolation (which also entailed an almost total sexual dysfunction) is related in the following incident. Playing instrumental music quite loudly on a powerful portable radio in the streets, he loved to "impose, as it were, this music on the passersby as if he were serenading them, as if perhaps he, and not the radio, made the music; and any theme, any motif, any phrase, any measures, truly seemed to him so much better if a pretty girl listened to these sounds while passing" (p. 228). Wolfson's second book is in fact such a serenade: somewhat like Allen Ginsberg's poem "Howl," it is a secular *Kaddish,* a lamentation, for his dead mother.

Ma mère, musicienne, est morte . . ., also written in French, bears as its full title *Ma mère, musicienne, est morte de maladie maligne mardi à minuit au milieu du mois de mai mille 977 au mouroir Memorial à Manhattan.*[2] Already, the consonance of the title reveals the continuation of Wolfson's concern with the *musication* of language, yet his manias now differed. As Wolfson explained, the name *Memorial Hospital* foretold the worst: this book was to be written *In memoriam!*, stressing the new, morbid significance foreshadowed by the title of his mother's favorite tune, "Good Night Ladies." Now, he had abandoned his linguistic analyses, though not his hatred of the English language, for a new obsession: horse racing. Yet this would permit him to continue his linguistic studies in a quite different manner, in accordance with his personal system for winning at the track. For example, he went to the races on the twelfth anniversary of President Kennedy's death, and explained the interest in betting on the following horses: "*Eurêka!* was the drama in Dallas twelve years ago"; "*Gun Toter*—a specifically American expression meaning 'Pistol or Revolver Bearer' "; "*Bye Bye Skipa* ("Bye Boss"); "*K's Image* (K for Kennedy)"; *Shannon M* (the Irish river, and Kennedy was of Irish origins)"; and so on. As his earlier narrative was punctuated by phonetic inventions and analyses, this later book is punctuated by such accounts of his betting at the races.

But there is a second, and more profound, linguistic interweaving in this text. His mother, who died a terrible death of cancer, kept a detailed diary of her illness. Translated selections from this diary are added to Wolfon's own account of her death; and in fact, he claimed that, "My book has a double title and two authors: *Ma mère, musicienne, est morte . . .* or *Exterminez l'Amérique,* by Rose Minarsky & Louis Wolfson." Whereas in *Le Schizo et les langues* Wolfson accentuated all that he needed to do to separate himself from his mother, in *Ma mère, musicienne, est morte . . .* he strived toward an ultimate reconciliation and attachment, to the extent that at one point he even made a syntactic error entailing the confusion of his self and his mother: "Tuesday, during the day, my mother complained me [*se me plaignait*] a couple of times about feeling an abdominal pain upon getting off of the bus" (p. 11). Both the curious construction *se me plaignait* and the unidiomatic use of *une couple* express his new-found attachment to, and identification with, his mother. He went even further: in hearing that his mother's cancer began in her ovaries, Wolfson claimed, "I vaguely thought that I too equally began, so to speak, in the ovary" (p. 86). He identified with his mother, with her pain, her disease, her death.

It is precisely the conditions of her death that brought mother and son together through a series of ironies. Now it is the mother who is confined to the hospital, as the son was before incarcerated in psychiatric institutions; now the earphones of his Walkman are called stethoscopes; now his music triumphs—no longer needed as a defense against the mother—whereas her singing voice, her organ playing, are stilled.

Wolfson and his mother, as well as their two texts, are joined by death, which forever silences. The rewritten, definitive version of *Le Schizo et les langues,* completed before the death of his mother, was rebaptized *Point finale à une planète infernale.* This retitling, along with the apocalyptic pronouncements in *Ma mère, musicienne, est morte . . .,* are his means of coming to terms with the suffering (his own and his mother's) of life and the incomprehensibility of death. Bewailing the ills of the world, he saw the only possible cure in a total radioactive sterilization of the planet, a "planetary euthanasia," a "supercolossal collective Bang!" (p. 22). He cited the Bible in explanation: "there shall be an end to death, and to mourning and crying and pain; for the old order has passed away! (*Apocalypse,* XXI, 4)" (p. 109).

Perhaps in response to his mother's use of the exclamation, "Mon Dieu!" ("My God!"), Wolfson occasionally utilized as an expletive the phrase, "Milles bombes!" ("A Thousand Bombs!") Once, when finding a rabbi at his mother's hospital bedside, Wolfson blurted out, "Dieu est la Bombe!" ("God is the bomb!"), which, though upsetting and incomprehensible to the rabbi, is in fact perfectly consistent with Wolfson's millenarian ideals. The book ends: "I obviously do not know how many millions, billions, nonillions (is this even a finite number?) of planets suffered a true nuclear euthanasia that night of 17 and 18 May 1977, but, quite unfortunately, the Earth was not (yet?) among them!" (p. 201). His paranoid, defensive, internalized use of music as an isolation mechanism *(Le schizo et les langues)* has been exteriorized and aggrandized, giving way to the even more paranoid desire for an apocalyptic atomic "big bang," to be followed by the infinite silence of universal death. Has a more touching eulogy ever been written?

What if the guiding principle of the cosmos were music? What if music were the fundamental element of the soul? The case of Adolf Wölfli is one of the most extreme manifestations of paranoid obsessions structured by an arcane cosmology.[3] Specific to this cosmology is the significant role of music as a symbolic and pragmatic element. Perhaps not since the Pythagoreans has music played such a dominant role in a *Weltanschauung*. Pythagorean philosophy (approximately 500 B.C.) had as its ultimate aim the contemplation and understanding of the Music of the Spheres. In a conceptual system whose central tenet was "All is number," this celestial music was the ultimate cosmological structure, consisting of the harmonic relations between the varied geometric orbits of the celestial bodies—music as celestial algebra. This is a metaphor that is to recur throughout the Western theological tradition.

Among the first signatures utilized by Wölfli we find in 1904: "A.W.—Adolf Wölfli. Composer," and perhaps the most descriptive is that used in 1908: "Drawer,—Poet,—Scribe,—COMPOSER,—Allgebrahtor,—Patient,—cast-off accident,—casualty,—grim casualty,—Doufi." At least on the quotidian level of his life in the Waldau asylum, these qualifications described his earthly existence. They also described the varied aspects of his creative activity, where image, music, and word form a unified *Gesamtkunstwerk.* [figures 15–18] Yet the signature of "St. Adolf" is no less important, denoting the core of his spiritual life with its constant cosmic voyages and ecstatic martyrdoms. For Wölfli, the quotidian and the spiritual were never dissociated: the paranoid systematization of experience entails a conceptual and emotional organization that excludes all accident and creates a fully integrated symbolic system in which all elements are inextricably interrelated. Everything is essential to the system, constant interchanges of elements occur, and there is no room for "dead time" or for empty spaces.

Wölfli's claim that "Algebra is music!" does not even begin to explain this system, which must be considered in terms of the extreme limits of obsessive, anguished, repetitive acts. The *horror vacui* common to many artworks created by paranoids reaches its apotheosis not only in Wölfli's work, but also in his life. His logorrhea, melomania, and iconophilia all serve to reduce the anguish that gripped him. His hyperbolic use of numbers, music, words, and images—all organized according to paratactic relations, tending toward extension to infinity—serve as means of both filling in the material emptiness of his isolated

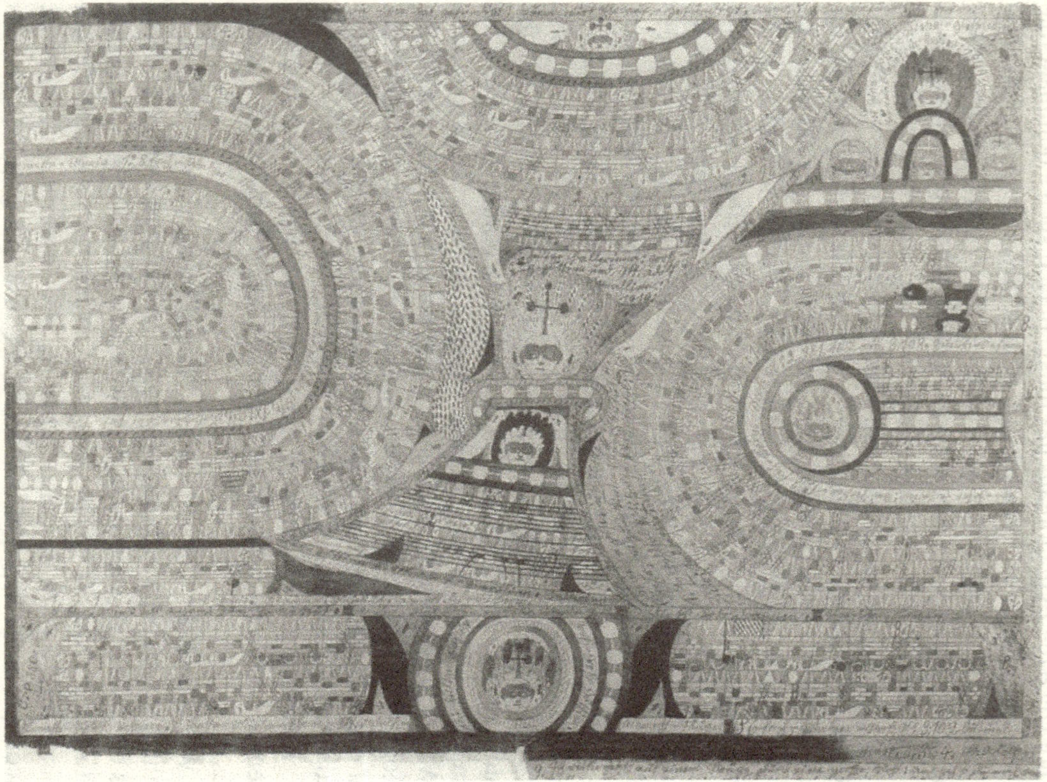

Figure 15. Adolf Wölfli, "Die heilige Ballerinna: Gross-Gross-Göttinn und, Skt. Adolf, Gemahlinn," 1916 (photo courtesy the Adolf Wölfli Foundation, Kunstmuseum Bern).

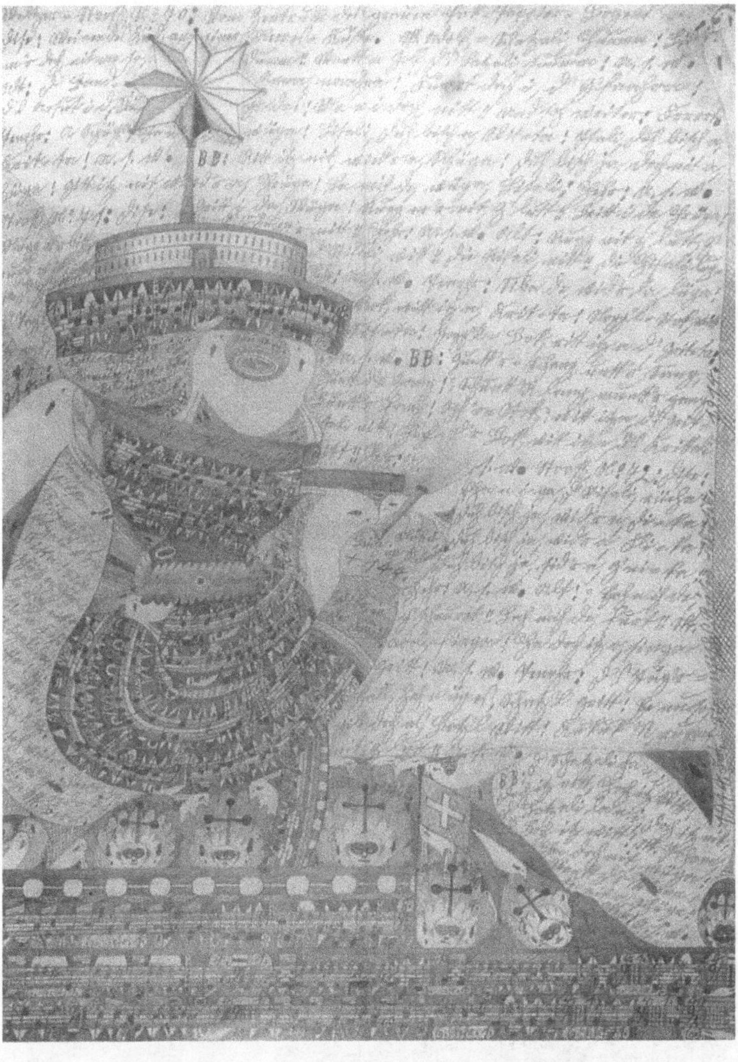

Figure 16. Adolf Wölfli, "Chaami-Zünd-Holtz-Fabrik," 1914 (photo courtesy the Adolf Wölfli Foundation, Kunstmuseum Bern).

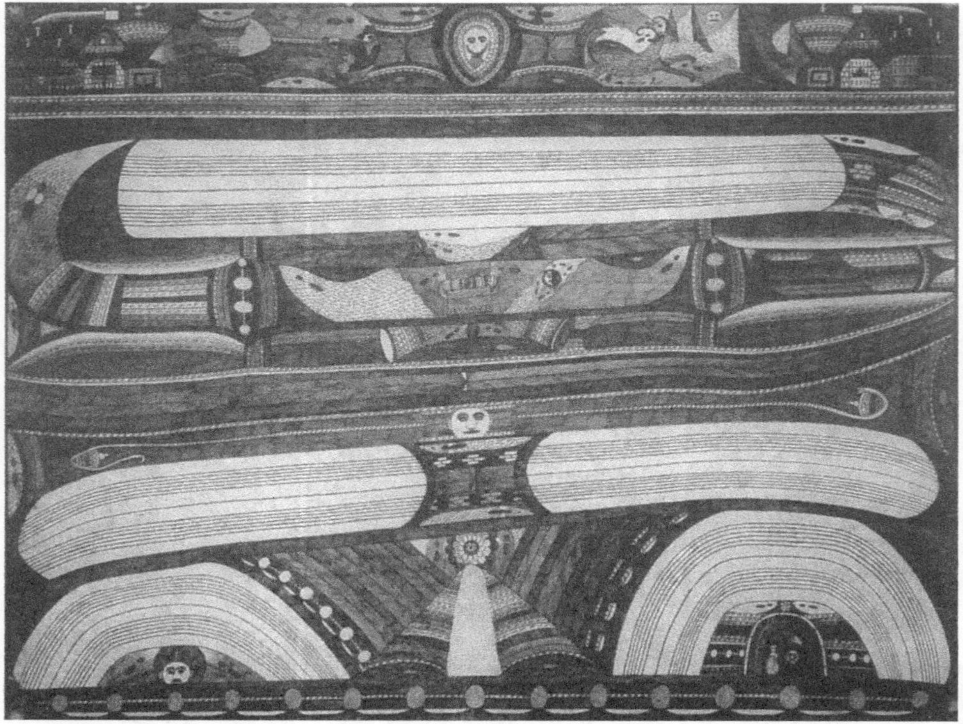

Figure 17. Adolf Wölfli, "Petrrohl, 1904 (photo courtesy the Adolf Wölfli Foundation, Kunstmuseum Bern).

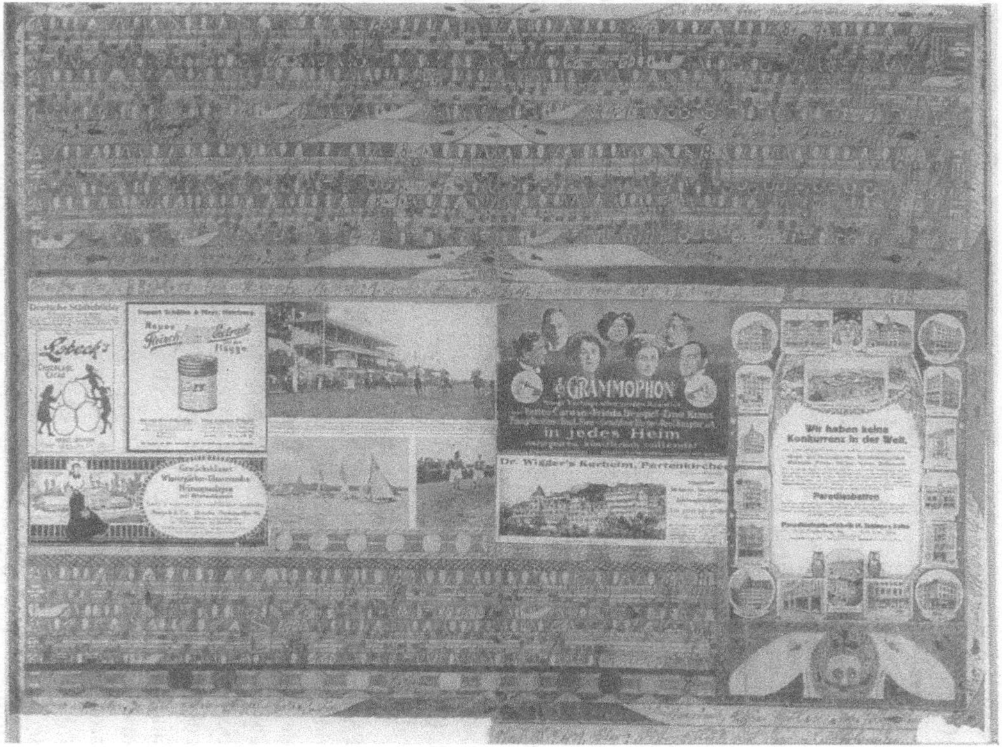

Figure 18. Adolf Wölfli, "Grammophon," 1915 (photo courtesy the Adolf Wölfli Foundation, Kunstmuseum Bern).

existence and reducing the anguish and terror of his all too full paranoid spiritual manifestations. His entire work is a sort of apotropaic incantation, simultaneously creating a cosmos *and* avoiding its catastrophic destruction (or, in psychological terms, achieving a certain amount of ego stability).

Wölfli suffered from auditory hallucinations typical of paranoid schizophrenia. For Wölfli, these sounds are ambiguously symbolized by the *vögeli,* the birds, that often serve as pictorial filler material in his drawings. Wölfli was tormented by voices, spoke with them, argued and ranted against them—but did not succumb. He answered the "din of the celestial birds" with a cosmological music of his own. Was music ultimately his foremost defense against, or rather a sublimation of, these voices?

Wölfli's case was not unique. In *Memoirs of My Nervous Illness,* the psychotic paranoid Daniel Paul Schreber explained how the destruction of his reason was in part effected by the *miraculated birds:* mainly composed of songbirds, such as swallows, sparrows, and crows, Schreber claimed that he never encountered one that was not endowed with speech! These miraculated birds did not at all comprehend the meaning of the words they pronounced, but spoke rather in pure homphonies, sounds with which Schreber's own nerves painfully vibrated. Schreber's ultimate defense against this ornithological *bruitage* was music:

> Playing the piano and reading books and newspapers is—as far as the state of my head allows—my main defense, which makes even the most drawn-out voices finally perish; at night when this is not easily done or in day-time when the mind requires a change of occupation, I usually found committing poems to memory a successful remedy. I learnt a great number of poems by heart, particularly Schiller's ballads, long sections of Schiller's and Geothe's dramas, as well as arias from operas and humorous poems, amongst others from *Max and Moritz, Struwelpeter,* and Spekter's fables, which I then recite in silence on the quiet verbatim. Their value as poetry naturally does not matter; however insigificant the rhymes, even obscene verses are worth their weight in gold as mental nourishment compared with the terrible nonsense my nerves are otherwise forced to listen to.[4]

Whereas Schreber's musical defense mechanism reveals his cultured origins (Schreber was a Senatspräsident in Leipzig), Wölfli's choice of musical idioms belies his lowly origins: songs, polkas, mazurkas, waltzes, and marches. Here, we cannot deny the often ritual or magical aspects at the origins of much folk music, transformed into Wolfli's incantations. He performed this music by blowing into horns consisting of rolled-up paper, practicing phrases many times until he attained a satisfactory rendition, with the results often sounding akin to country brass band music. The techniques of Wölfli's poetics and music were in fact quite similar to the music of Schreber's birds: in Wölfli's poetry, words were chosen not primarily for their meaning, but rather for their rhythmic, rhymed, and sonorous effects, and words were disarticulated into syllables and letters, only to be rearticulated into often senseless neologisms. In Wölfli's music, full of phonetic rhymes and solmizations, rhythm is essential, and numerous variations on a single melody might be performed in different registers. Once the piece was perfected, it was written down.

Just as Wölfli's music was an integral factor of his cosmology, his musical notation was an integral factor in his drawings, serving not only as musical notation, but also as decorative elements, figurative components (through an extreme plasticity of the figurative apparatus, the musical notation is at times transformed into figurative elements, such as the tail of a comet), and even as sheer filler, like the birds themselves. Like every element in Wölfli's art, there is a precarious balance between figuration and ornamentation, leading toward an extreme schematization or mannerism; and like every element in his work (especially the numerical calculations and the textual narratives), there is no beginning or end, just a continual addition of elements.

As musical notation, Wölfli's transcriptions are practically illegible. Yet this must not be taken as a sign of incapacity, but rather as a structural feature of the relations between his music and his cosmos. Although there is a maximal determinacy in his musical performance (based on the popular genres that form the basis of his music: polkas, mazurkas, marches, waltzes, etc.), there is a minimal determinacy in his musical notation.[5] These scores, the veritable simulacra of standard musical notation, contain minimal, ambiguous information, tending toward, but not quite attaining, full musical sense. These musical scores constitute a discourse that hides its secrets; they signify a purely performative system, where there can be no differentiation between composer and performer, a private musical language, based on stereotyped musical genres. Whereas the parameters of this music are apparent to us, its nuances—connoted but never denoted by the notation—exist for Wölfli and Wölfli alone. These highly graphic scores are thus open systems, open scores, based on a highly structured typification of styles necessitating extremely limited performance possibilities—a sort of *musique pauvre*. What are for us the indeterminate, aleatory, improvisatory implications of his scores were for Wölfli just the opposite: his music was never truly improvised, created *ex improviso* (i.e., without preparation) because his entire cosmological system, his entire oeuvre, was the basis for his music. Paranoia eliminates all accidents in life, transforming the accidental into the essential by an overdetermination of the meaning of each and every object and event. For Wölfli, the only place left for the accidental might in fact have been in the open-ended musical and mathematical systems. Yet even here, the function of addition ultimately incorporates all accident, every new bit of information or event, into the closed cosmic system by means of a paratactic paranoid accumulation.

There is, though, one point of total emptiness, sheer indeterminacy, absolute silence in his work: many of his drawings contain empty musical staffs, devoid of notes or images. These staffs fill the empty space with the sign for silence—do they as such signify that death which was to be the theme of his final work, *The Funeral March?* Or is this merely the ubiquitous silence that serves as the precondition for all music, as John Cage has taught us? [figure 17]

It would be an error to consider Wölfli's music as part of the continuum of the Western musical tradition, given that his music is ruled by the particularities of his paranoid thought (just as is every element of his everyday life). And yet, it might be useful to cite several parallels between his musical innovations and those of modern music—yet most of these innovations and experimentations were predated by Wölfli.

1. *Birdsong*. The work of Olivier Messiaen has been most deeply influenced by his study of birdsong. *Messe de la Pentecôte* (1950), one of his major compositions, contains the following movements: *Les Langues de Feu, Les Choses visibles et invisibles, Le Don de sagesse, Les Oiseaux et les Sources, Le Vent de l'Esprit*. The events of Pentacost—that is, the descent of the Holy Spirit, manifested in glossolalic speaking in tongues—here suggest the

equation of birdsong, glossolalia, and the "wind of the spirit." Note also his works *Le Merle noir* (1952), *Oiseaux exotiques* (1955), *Catalogue d'oiseaux* (1956–1958), *La Fauvette des jardins* (1970).

2. *Folk music*. The musical compositions of Béla Bartok and Zoltån Kodaly abound in citations of Eastern European folk music, much of which they transcribed and collected, as for example Bartok's *Rumanian Folk Dances* and *Hungarian Folksongs*. Earlier manifestations of the integration of folk into classical music would include Tchaikovsky, Dvořák, Grainger, and D'Indy, among others.
3. *Indeterminate and aleatory music*. The role of chance in musical composition and performance was pioneered by such innovators as John Cage, Karlheinz Stockhausen, Morton Feldman, and Luciano Berio. And we should note, of course, the improvisatory element of jazz.
4. *Graphic scores*. Avant garde improvisation occasionally reaches the extreme limit of indeterminacy where the performer is virtually the composer—here, the score may contain absolutely minimal information, so that total improvisation is the only possibility. Thus varying amounts of musical information, notated in varying degrees of ambiguity, may be used to channel improvisation. This leeway permits the creation of graphic scores, which serve simultaneously as musical scores and graphic artworks; for example, Sylvano Bussotti's *Five Pieces for David Tudor* (1959), and his *La Passion selon Sade* (1966); John Cage's *Water Music* (1952; incidentally, some of Cage's performances also contain bird calls); and Karlheinz Stockhausen's *Kontakte* (1958–1960).

These modern musical experiments, and many others, shattered traditional musical forms; it is only within this expanded understanding of music that we can begin to retrospectively understand, and appreciate, Wölfli's own music. But, as a necessary counterpoint, we must also consider it within the rubrics of psychoanalytic and cultural studies of schizophrenia, for it is within the "split" soul that such a music as Wölfli's can occur.

We also find analogous parallels with modernist poetry. Wölfli's texts are interspersed with tone poems, such as the following cradle song:

G'ganggali ging g'gang, g'gung g'ung!
Giigara-Lina Wiiy Rosina.
G'ganggali ging g'ang, g'gung g'gung!
Rittara-Gritta, d'Zittara witta.
G'ganggali ging g'gang, g'ung g'gung.
Giigaralina, siig'R a Fina.
G'ganggali ging g'gang, g'ung g'gung!
Fung z'Jung, chung d'Stung.[6]

Wölfli's *magnum opus, The Funeral March,* contains both birds and music. It is a dirge and love song of pain and suffering, hope and wisdom. We can never know the full meaning of *The Funeral March,* for it was sung by Wölfli alone, for Wölfli alone, a sort of autistic music. And yet, is it not precisely in such works that autism becomes communicative and that we reach the inner recesses of another's soul? Is it not only in such extreme cases that we can even begin to imagine the depths of another's soul, as well as of our own? How, indeed, do *we* sing? For whom? And against what?

TEN

Radiophonic Art: The Voice of the Impossible Body

> Isn't it blasphemy to reserve this mouth to and in and out of breathing, to the drudgery of absorbing food, and the golden middle of this magnificent behind to the sad labor of discharging excrement. Can this tongue move only syllables and dead matter.
>
> —*Heiner Müller*
> *Quartet*

Rabelais, in the fourth book of *Pantagruel,* described a seafaring voyage during which the crew hears voices that seem to come from thin air, an effect causing great fear. Pantagruel explained that these sounds consist of words that were frozen in the winter air and that begin to thaw out on being touched, thus becoming audible.

> And we could see sharp words, bloody words (which, according to the pilot, sometimes went back to the place where they'd been spoken, only to find the throat that uttered them had been slit open), horrible words, and many others equally unpleasant to see. And when they'd melted, we heard: *hin, hin, hin, hin, hiss, tick, tock, whizz, gibber, jabber, frr, frrr, frrr, boo, boo, boo, boo, boo, boo, boo, boo, crack, track, trr, trr, trr, trrr, trrrrr, on, on, on, on, wooawooawoooon, gog, magog,* and God only knows what other barbarian words.[1]

Though his companions wished to preserve some of these words in oil, Pantagruel said that it is not worth saving what is always plentifully at hand. Can we not see in this scenario the phantasm at the origins of radiophonic art, where the word is embalmed and speech immortalized? Only the slit throat, the terminal loss of body, indeed death, permits an eternal return of the voice. The French playwright Valère Novarina explained the extreme difficulty in reading Rabelais, a difficulty described in terms of a veritable archaeology of the lived, respiratory, musculatory, enunciatory patterns of the French language. "To read him is to change bodies; it is an act of respiratory exchange, it is to breathe within another's body."[2] Believing in the interlocutory presence of the lived body, Novarina is truly a man of the theater, and he consequently provided a critique of present day mainstream radio:

> They work night and day with immense teams and enormous financial means: a cleansing of the body in sound recording, a toilet of the voice, filtering, tapes edited and carefully purified of all laughs, farts, hiccoughs, salivations, respirations, of all the slag that marks the animal, material nature of the words that come from the human body . . .[3]

He proposed, in its stead, a new use of the voice that harkens back to Artaud's own transformation of the vocal arts:

> Mouth, anus. Sphincters. Round muscles closing our holes. The opening and the closing of the word. Attack cleanly (teeth, lips, muscled mouth) and finish cleanly (cut off the air). Stop cleanly. Chew and eat the text. A blind spectator should be able to hear it crunched and swallowed, to ask himself what is being eaten over there, on stage. What are they eating? They're eating themselves? Chewing or swallowing. Mastication, sucking, swallowing. Pieces of the text must be bitten off, viciously attacked by the female eaters (lips, teeth); other pieces must be quickly gulped down, swallowed, gobbled up, breathed in, guzzled. Eat, gulp, eat, chew, dry lung, chew, masticate, cannibal![4]

Certainly apparent in the productions of Novarina's own theater, there are indeed also radiophonic works that instantiate this recorporealization of the human voice—all the while achieving a disquieting grafting of mechanical, electric, and electronic possibilities onto the strictly human potentials of sound recording and transmissions—an artificial transmogrification of respiratory patterns and vocal intonations.[5]

Novarina informed us that, "Since the age of zero I have always had the impression of carrying my skull like a pebble within my thought."[6] We should take such new corporeal paradigms seriously and literally. The spoken words of one's own voice resonate through the entire body, originating in the diaphragm, larynx, and mouth and resounding through the jaws and cranium before ever reentering through the ears. I live my own voice as a simultaneous density of bodily overtones—the tonal center is a vibratory resonance between the pitch of my body and the echoes of my speech returned by the world. The recorded voice, the phonographic voice, the radiophonic voice, the played back voice of our own enunciations universally creates a certain disquietude, for this voice arrives from without, minus its usual corporeal thickness; such a voice is "deboned."[7] Needless to say, for me the other's voice is always already "deboned," as all enunciations foreign to my own come from outside. There is a structural solipsism to the enunciatory mechanism, regulated by the corporeal parallax between speech and audition. The inherent mystery of the incarnate other is such that, as Novarina insisted, "all words are scars of the spirit."[8] The spoken voice creates a wound; the recorded voice produces an ever visible scar. Scars of the spirit, or of the body, or of the tape.[9]

With the practice of sound recording and editing, we discover the technodream of musical perfectibility. Glenn Gould's legendary text, "The Prospects of Recording," outlines both the effects of recording on musical composition *and* the utopian limits of musical possibility established by electronic sound reproduction. The influence of recording paradigms on modern musical *composition* includes "the reiterated note pattern, with measured crescendo and diminuendo; the dynamic comparison between close-up and far-distant statements of the same configuration; the quasimechanical ritard or accelerando; above all, the possibility of a controlled release and attack of sound."[10] But recording has also changed the very patterns and expectations of musical *listening*. Musical performance is now associated with a new extreme of "analytic clarity, immediacy, and indeed almost tactile proximity" (certainly in part a compensatory mechanism for the total loss of visual perception in the sound recording process);[11] microphonic sensitivity has created both instrumental balances and sound discriminations unavailable in live symphonic spaces; listener control of sophisticated, ultrasensitive home stereophonic equipment permits subtle gradations within an infinite set of different playback "performances" (thus establishing the listener as a composer after the fact, complicating the entire question of authorship, where the composer, like the sound, becomes a function of mixing); and an ideal or utopian performance becomes possible by splicing together different musical entities to create an optimum effect, as in Gould's example of a high C sung by Elisabeth Schwarzkopf that is appended to Kirsten Flagstad's part in a certain recording of *Tristan*.[12] Finally, we can even recompose entire symphonies utilizing this recombinatory technique, as in Gould's example of the possibility of editing together Bruno Walter's performance of the exposition and recapitulation of the first movement of Beethoven's Fifth Symphony with Klemperer's handling of the development section.[13]

The recombinatory possibilities suggested by the new musical paradigms instituted by Gould gave rise not only to a new mode of music and musication, but also to a new dimension of the human voice. Perhaps Schwarzkopf would consider Gould's vocal tamperings utopian; Whitehead would probably call them monstrous. For recording and radiophonic art permit the creation of not only ideal, but also impossible, vocal articulations. The hybrid Schwarzkopf-Flagstad creature is a primal example; more intricate is Gregory Whitehead's *If a voice like, then what?*, where we are asked whether our voice resembles a composite recorded sound that could not possibly exist as a single human enunciation. The sound in fact consists of hundreds of recorded samplings of Whitehead's own voice, both spoken normally and distorted through megaphones, then cut up, fragmented, damaged, and finally sutured through four-track mixing. Might we presume that this voice exists in the subjunctive mood of radiophony, a sound that is never truly heard? Such monsters exist both within the recorded voice *and* in the realm of the putative ideal listener, as is expressed by the following anecdote describing the early years of sound recording in the cinema. At that time (the 1930s), several microphones were normally scattered around the set to capture all sounds, and afterward the signals were mixed in the studio to obtain a consistent, coherent, intelligible sound and speech quality. Yet there was an inherent discrepancy between the unique visual camera viewpoint and the multifarious positioning of the microphones, such that the auditory aspect of the spectacle was fragmented and only artificially recombined. In an early article, one critic described the paradoxical spectatorial position in relation to these films: "When a number of microphones are used, the resultant blend of sound may not be said to represent any given point of audition, but is the sound which would be heard by a man with five or six very long ears, said ears extending in various directions."[14] This was a confusion of media, caused by the commixture of the radio industry and the film industry. Whereas radio broadcasting of the epoch sought to present all sounds as coming from approximately the same spatial plane, the film industry needed to create spatial effects through auditory means. The logic of this visualized spatiality necessitated the representation of a unified and nonfragmented body, of the sort that reigns today in mainstream narrative radio and cinema, due to the widespread suturing effects of iconic, narrative, and representational structures.

But there is another body, fragmented, schizoid, "the limbo of a nightmare of bones and muscles."[15] Just before his death in 1948, Antonin Artaud created his major radiophonic work, *Pour en finir avec le jugement de dieu (To Have Done with the Judgement of God)*. Artaud's decade-long internment in psychiatric institutions—where he suffered a spiritual, symbolic, metaphysical "death," as he so often claimed—corresponded with the duration of World War II. Perhaps the terrible manifestations of war—the shrieks of sirens, screams, shattered and dismembered bodies, the explosions of bombs, countless ways of dying—were psychically displaced by Artaud, expressed in his subsequent aesthetic mannerisms as well as in the more immediate morbid symptoms of his paranoid schizophrenic illness. His behavior in the asylum was characterized by delusions, auditory hallucinations, repetitive ritualistic acts, coprophilia, glossolalia, violent uncontrollable tantrums, and so on. The therapeutic response was equally violent: electroshock and insulin shock therapies. (We might mention, without further comment, that electroshock therapy, creating violent convulsions of the body, was developed in Rome in 1938; insulin shock therapy, which puts the body in a comatose state, was developed in Vienna in 1933.) Would it be too extravagant to suggest that those electric shocks which traversed and convulsed Artaud's body were countered by electric "shocks" of his own: a radiophonic transmission intended not only to save the spirit, but also to transform the body?[16] *Pour en finir avec le jugement de dieu* is the ultimate manifestation of Artaud's "theater of cruelty." In a letter of 1933, Artaud described his theatrical project in a manner that foreshadows his radiophonic work: "it must abandon individual psychology, enter into mass passions, into the conditions of the collective spirit, grasp the collective wavelengths, in short, change the subject" (V, 153). Furthermore, he speaks of "The theater as a bath of psychic electricity where the intellect will be periodically reimmersed" (IV, 321). The redemptive quality of such a work cannot be overlooked. In contrast to the demonic (and human) voices that had tormented him, he could now broadcast and thus universalize his own passions, his final revenge. Yet recording the voice always poses a distinct ontological risk: the recorded voice is the stolen voice, which returns to the speaker as the hallucinatory, disembodied presence of another. This other's voice may be the voice of God—the acousmetric voice: ubiquitous, panoptic, omniscent, omnipotent—as is so often the case in paranoid schizophrenic projections.[17] These projections produce a divine or diabolical presence miraculously speaking forbidden thoughts or unspeakable desires or unbearable prohibitions. Did the event of recording *Pour en finir avec le jugement de dieu* (the broadcast of which was ultimately suppressed) effect the exorcism of God as Artaud intended? Or was it in fact the last instance of that tragic irony of Artaud's struggle with God, where God triumphed over Artaud once again, just before his death, by stealing his voice only to definitively separate it from his body become corpse? Is it Artaud's voice that we hear, or is this but one more manifestation of the voice of divine judgment?

Artaud's use of the radio led him to thematize an impossible, monstrous body, evoked precisely to escape from the "limbo of a nightmare of bones and muscles," to circumvent and transcend what Bachelard spoke of as the "visceral imagination" or what Barthes wrote of as "the grain of the voice." This is the corporeal utopia of the "body without organs."

> From whatever angle one approaches you, you are mad, mad enough to be tied down. By having him undergo once more but for the last time a session on the autopsy table in order to remake his anatomy. I say, in order to remake his anatomy. Man is sick because he is badly constructed. We must decide to strip him in order to scratch out this animalcule which makes him itch to death, god, and with god, his organs. For tie me down if you want to, but there is nothing more useless than an organ. When you have given him a body without organs, then you will have delivered him from all his automatisms and restored him to his true liberty.[18]

The "body without organs" is the ultimate "deboning" of the voice, a recreation or disarticulation of the corporeal structure that takes on cosmic dimensions. It is thus no accident that this corporeal phantasm first arises in conjunction with a radiophonic work, radio being the site par excellence for such anatomical revisions, and ultimately for the loss of the body. In "Interjections," the opening section of *Suppôts et supplications* (1946), we find a total renunciation of existence expressed in a diffuse and all-encompassing series of negations, including

> no mind, no soul, no heart, no family, no families of being, no legions, no confraternities, no participation, no communion of saints, no angels, no beings, no dialectic, no logic, no syllogistics, no ontology, no rule, no regulations, no law, no universe, no conception, no notion, no concepts, no affects, no tongue, no uvula, no glottis, no glands, no thyroid organs, no organs, no nerves, no veins, no bones . . . (XIV**, 13).

This rejection of the world, an implicit rejection of all possible genealogy (especially of the Oedipal "papa-mama"), reveals the desire to escape all "anxiety of influence" by becoming one's own origin and telos. Neither microcosm nor macrocosm is spared. Not only is this body without organs psychotically necessary to prevent the penetration of the body by evil physical and metaphysical beings and forces, not only does it seal the body and prevent the escape and theft of words and thoughts, not only does it entail an aesthetic dissent against the entire history of representation, but it is also symbolically necessary to protest against the phallicization of the body, where any organ or limb can be transmuted into a phallic substitute. For the phallic body is a body in conflict with itself: because the phallus can be symbolized by any other body part, symbolically displaced onto any organ, the body *with* organs evinces a perilous instability, always susceptible to historical and theological vaguaries, to the judgments of men and God. Those who were castrated by the Church to modulate the voice and create more beautiful musical tones, those whose tongues were cut out by the State to silence their protest, those who were granted prosthetic devices by the medical profession (like the artificial voice box of the man who spoke the computer's voice in Godard's *Alphaville*) to compensate for physical losses and cancerous damages—none can even hint at the implications of the body without organs.

Writing of the historical incorporation of phonetics into linguistics, Roman Jakobson cited a text that describes, "a particular laryngal articulation which would, had this description been accurate, have inevitably resulted in the fatal strangulation of the speaker."[19] Yet this error is but a hyperbolic statement of the truth pertaining to the expression of anger. The state of anger or hatred considerably increases muscular tension; in regard to its verbal expression, the psycholinguist Ivan Fónagy explained:

> We also observe that anger and especially hatred prolong the duration of the occlusion, and narrow the buccal canal during the articulation of frictive consonants. The evidence of glottal tomography is even clearer and more decisive. Following a hyperfunction of the sphincter muscles of the glottis, the passage of air becomes difficult. Aggressive or hateful phonation often produces a *strangled* voice. This metaphor contains the key to the explication of the gesture: one strangles oneself in order to prefigure homicide. According to a magical conception of the world, this would operate as an action that would in itself suffice to eliminate the adversary.[20]

Yet on the psychophonetic level, this sort of expression is doomed to failure, because when anger erupts the vocal cords are not sufficiently close together to vibrate, and in suppressed anger they are too tightly compressed to vibrate normally. The result of such violent muscular contractions is often a state where the vibrations of the vocal cords are "replaced by the sound of air turbulence—a *flatus vocis*—passing through the narrowed glottis."[21] An essential element of the expression of anger or hatred is the simultaneous stimulation and contraction of antagonistic muscle groups in the body. These conflicts are more than metaphoric: they express the profoundly heterogeneous functioning of what normally appears to be a unified, holistic body, a gestalt organization of the corporeal sensorium. Certain psychopathological conditions raise this heterogeneity—what is all too often viewed as a sort of dysfunction—to a higher and more explicit level, such as in the phantasms of *disjecta membra* characteristic of schizophrenia. Artaud:

> man does not live through his entire self at each instant of his body, in an absolute space of the body; he is sometimes knee and sometimes foot, sometimes occiput and sometimes ear, sometimes lungs and sometimes liver, sometimes membrane and sometimes uterus, sometimes anus and sometimes nose, sometimes sex and sometimes heart, sometimes saliva and sometimes urine, sometimes aliment and sometimes sperm, sometimes excrement and sometimes idea; what I mean is that the ego or the self is not centered on a unique perception, and that the ego is not unique be-

> cause it is dispersed throughout the body instead of the body being gathered around itself in an absolute sensorial equality, comprising a perception of the absolute. For man is not only *dispersed* throughout his body, he is also dispersed in the outside of things, like a corpse who forgot his own body . . . (XI, 103–104).

We find in Artaud the conflict between the ideal of a body without organs and the reality of a body with too many organs. This corporeal and cosmic, schizoid and carnivalesque multiplication and confusion of organs is at the core of Artaud's poetics. He asks the question: "isn't the mouth of the current human race, following the anatomical survey of the present human body, this hole of being situated just at the outlet of the hemorrhoids of Artaud's ass?" (XIV**, 153). This scabrous affront of conflating or juxtaposing mouth and anus is more than metaphorical; psycholinguistics teaches us that the glottic sphincter achieves the physical and symbolic articulation of oral and anal functions by means of glottal occlusives. These often choking sounds, created by the closure of the glottis, establish a subglottal pressure on the diaphragm and intestines, thus facilitating defecation. This determines a desublimatory trajectory from sublimated speech to the inner depths of the body: the web of the symbolic ends in the bowels. For someone like Artaud, who died of rectal cancer, such as realignment of the body politic is of mortal import.[22]

Is this vocal malleability and transferability, its metastatic character, perhaps the gist of the question asked by Gregory Whitehead's radiophonic piece, *Oral or Anal?* This work consists of the recitation of all combinations of the syllables in its title. Does *Oral or Anal?* pose a question about sexuality, about the eroticism of a normal body *with* organs? Is it an exclusive or inclusive disjunction, imposing a sexual injunction? Or does it rather bespeak the manifest impossibility (but distinct, if perverse, radiophonic possibility) of *organs without a body?* Or consider Whiteheads's work *The Problem with Bodies,* where we are asked to repeat the proposition "The problem with bodies is the reason for antibodies, and the problem with antibodies is no body at all," first without using our tongues, then without opening our mouths, and finally without using our larynx. We might indeed say that the problem with bodies cannot truly be expressed, because the body is neither purely natural nor purely textual, but rather the primal symbolic system that articulates nature and culture. As transformed by the rerecording, looping, and feedback capabilities of sound engineering (especially given the subliminal, microphonic levels of digital sampling), the human voice in radiophonic art (and, by extension, in certain extreme examples of experimental cinema) will project the voice of "nobody," which like Artaud's "body without organs" is proposed as an antidote to the ills that beset the fragile, tortured body in pain.[23] We must therefore rethink the radio in terms of another articulatory—or rather disarticulatory—site of the symbolic, not representing the body but rather *transforming* or *annihilating* it.

The phantasm of a body without organs radically disrupts the very forms of our discourse. The same might be said for the phantasm of a body with too many organs, or a deformed body with hypertrophied or hypotrophied organs. Such a Rabelasian body might incite a confusion of tongues to match the intracorporeal battle—the antagonism or agony—of organs and muscle groups. Or it might invoke, as is the case in Valère Novarina's works, the form of litany, "to repeat the names until it causes a whirling drunkenness,"[24] which is comparable to Artaud's incantatory, exorcistic use of glossolalic language in his theater of cruelty. Consider Novarina's invention of 2,587 names in *Le drame de la vie* (the same number of names that appear in the Bible, exemplified by the genealogical lists in *Genesis* 5; 10; 11; 36; *Numbers* 26; *Chronicles I* 1–8.) The recitations of this litany constitute a primal creative act. Many of these "characters" speak only once; most never speak, or even appear, at all. They exist only through their names: existence is reduced to nomination, to pure connotation, without any possibility of description. Every such unique name is a hapax, a term existing but once in a lauguage, without origin or end, afterward forever lost. *Le drame de la vie* begins:

> The theater is empty. Adam enters.
>
> Adam. —How does it happen that one speaks? Let the meat express itself?
>
> He leaves. There enter the Man of Pontalambin, The Man of Lambi, John Membret, Sapolin, The Man of Saporleolimasse, Bandru, The Man of Pontagre, Bomberre, The Man of the Host . . .[25]

And so forth. It continues with numerous other names—or should we say nominative neologisms? This proliferation of names coincides with a reduction of bodies and entails a (perhaps compensatory) multiplication of grammatical moods and tenses:

> The antepositive accords in number with the gender of the preposition which its verb compliments; in the equalitive mode, as well as in the depreciative mode, the object of the subject remains blank. Recite the six modes that exist! The optional, the dictative, the subodorative, the injunctive, the inactive, the dodecational. The mode of separation is separative; the mode of options is the optional. Sixteen tenses exist while there is still time: the distant present, the advanced future, the inactive present, the disactive past, the more-than-present, its projective past, the posterior past, the worse-than-past, the never possible, the completed future, the terminated past, the possible anterior, the future posterior, the more-than-lost, the completative, the attentative.[26]

Given our new theatrical and radiophonic complexities and radical restructuring of the body, do we not need an indefinite number of novel tenses and grammatical modes, as vast as the figural and tropic possibilities being rediscovered by today's theoretical linguistics? Such aberrations reveal the madness of the imagination, the manifestation of difference in extremis. As each vocal monster bears a totally idiosyncratic structure, new grammatical, rhetorical, and poetic models are needed to describe such irregular, eccentric, heteromorphic discursive patterns.

In conclusion, we might consider the following tragic tale recounted by Novarina:

> I knew a man who swore every three sentences: "Fléau! Ah, fffléau!" [A plague! What a plague!] He hanged himself in the mountains one fine August day, after having repeated "fléau!" thirteen times in a row. . . . This man was like all the others: he wanted to risk being something other than his visible body, to reinvent another man in his place. It is quite unbearable for us to have but one head, feet down below, and only two arms.[27]

We could well imagine such a scene created by Robert Wilson or Heiner Müller or indeed by Novarina himself. But this is still theater, albeit culminating in silence. Were it radio, those words, his own, would eternally return to haunt the hanged man's grave, serving as his epitaph—reminding us of the prejudicial judgments of those men and gods that keep our own voices bound to but one body, indeed to narrowly restricted functions of the vocal cavity. It is only when our entire body becomes a mouth that we can truly speak. And even at that point, the radio will steal our voices, and send them back to us, impossible, monstrous enunciations—not a body without organs, but a voice without body, evoking an electroprosthetic resurrection beyond our most catastrophic destinies.

ELEVEN

Kinomadness

The dream of cinema has its origins in events as disparate as the paleolithic cave paintings of the Dordogne, where parietal animals seems to move in the flickering light of a fire; the ancient Greek philosophical phantasy of the shadow theater formed in Plato's cave; Cartesian automatons; seventeenth century Jesuit anamorphic representations and the images of their catoptric devices; the play of waters in the fountains of Versailles, and the spectacular fireworks of the royal court; nineteenth century dioramas, the birth of photography, and the invention of such protocinematic machines as the Zoetrope and the zoopraxiscope.

Consider also the dream of the cinema in a raindrop. Nature abounds in catoptric effects. In fact, every droplet of rain constitutes an elemental catoptric machine, due to the refractive properties of water. At the very origins of modern Western rationalism, René Descartes explained these principles in *Les Météores* (1637).[1] During a sunshower, for example, because of the slightly different refractive angle of each raindrop, the observor will witness a particular phenomenon of the transformation of sunlight: a rainbow. As Jurgis Baltrušaitus explained in *Le miroir:* "The rain of micro-mirrors reflects a deformed sun."[2] The most spectacular such effect is described in Book X of *Les Météores:* this is the apparition of several suns. During the occurrence of certain rare atmospheric conditions, cloud formations can refract sunlight so that as many as seven suns may be seen simultaneously. At such times, the sun may even appear to be transformed into the moon. At the end of the chapter of *Les Météores* entitled "On the Rainbow," Descartes utilized his study of these natural phenomena to describe how a mechanism could be invented for creating signs in the sky, according to the optical principles of the rainbow. A fountain could be constructed by utilizing several liquids of different viscosities (and thus of different refractive indexes) so that the light passing through it would be refracted according to precisely calculated degrees. This would create patterns in the sky, such as a cross or a column. We may see here the meteorological origins of the cinema.[3] Such dreams, and their empirical effects of the transformation of nature and the dispossession of the soul inspired their reactionary detractors. In the nineteenth century, Villiers de l'Isle Adam championed such a nostalgic, antitechnological position. His sardonic phantasies, nevertheless, were prophetic. In his tale, "L'Affichage céleste" (1873), Villiers satirized modern scientific technique by postulating the invention of the following machine: powerful jets of magnesium or electric light would project images magnified 100,000 times from the top of a hill onto the sky, or even onto the face of the moon.[4] The uses of such an invention, linked to the pictorial possibilities of the Lampascope (an early slide projector) are apparent: both advertising and politics would benefit. Villiers thus proposes an advertisement for liqueurs that would consist of the projected image of an angel holding a bottle in its hand, with a banderole coming out of its mouth bearing the words: "God, it's so good!" Another obvious practical use would be to project the images of criminals onto the clouds, thus facilitating their apprehension. The device could be made even more sophisticated: by means of a small wheel attached to the Lampascope, the expression of the projected faces could be modified, according to the changing needs of the spectacle. The importance of this invention is crucial in regard to the physiognomic mythos of the period, for we must remember that this was the last moment of the widespread belief in the scientific veracity of the relations between psychological character and physiognomic forms, where the form of the body reveals the truth of the soul. Yet, as we now know, the representations of the face must be understood as *symbols*, as a means of typification, and ultimately of stereotyping.

This criminological procedure coincides with the positivist influence on late nineteenth century criminology: Alphonse Berthillon's statistically based filing system within which photographic portraiture and anthropometric description were combined into an identificatory scheme (by means of juxtaposing photographs); and Francis Galton's creation of composite portraiture used to construct a pictorial typology of criminals (by the use of photographic superimposition).[5] These typologies resulted in the creation of images of idealized, standardized, stereotyped, nonexistent persons. In this merger of optics and statistics, we find an empirical application of the dreamwork: the processes of condensation, metonymic juxtaposition and physiognomization—in quest of the creation of the "average man"—are placed in the service of science, politics, and social control. Thus what would seem to be an empirical procedure is in fact a mode of pseudoscientific idealization. As Allan Sekula explained, "Galton, in seeking the apotheosis of the optical, attempted to elevate the indexical photographic composite to the level of the *symbolic,* thus expressing a *general law* through the accretion of contingent instances."[6] A contemporary aesthetic version of this procedure is worthy of notice. In the 1981, the filmmakers Helmut Lerch and Claus Holtz produced the work *Kopf,* created in a cinematic photomaton located in the Centre Georges Pompidou in Paris, within which the faces of countless visitors to the museum were each filmed for a few frames. Projected at normal speed, the kinetic superimposition or fusion of faces created an ideal face of asexual beauty, likened by some to that of a Raphaelesque angel. Here, the sum total of human physiognomic characteristics, the face of the "average" person, reveals the (bisexual or asexual) physiognomy of an angel! The cinematic apparatus forms part of the divine celestial mechanics.

The greatest meteorological artwork appears in the climax of the New Testament of the Bible, *The Revelation of John.* The apocalyptic opening of the seven seals disclosed the ultimate powers of the heavens over human destiny.

> There in heaven stood a throne, and on the throne sat one whose appearance was like the gleam of jasper and cornelian; and round the throne was a rainbow, bright as an emerald. In a circle about this throne were twenty-four other thrones, and on them sat twenty-four elders, robed in white and wearing crowns of gold. From the throne went out flashes of lightening and peals of thunder. Burning before the throne were seven flaming torches, the seven spirits of God, and in front of it stretched what seemed like a sea of glass, like a sheet of ice.[7]

The opening of the sixth, and penultimate, seal is noteworthy in this respect: "And there was a violent earthquake; the sun turned black as a funeral pall and the moon all red as blood; the stars in the sky fell to the earth, like figs shaken down by a gale; the sky vanished, as a scroll is rolled up."[8] Without psychologizing about the author of *The Revelation of John,* we need only point out the structural, textual, and affective similarities between theological apocalypses and the symptomatology of paranoid schizophrenia. Perhaps only in madness do we find the supreme conjunction of such optical, meteorological, theological, and cinematic phenomena. In Hans Prinzhorn's *Artistry of the Mentally Ill* (1922) (one of the first works to seriously treat the pictorial representations of the mentally ill as art) the work of a patient named August Neter is presented. In 1907, at the age of 39, Neter began to have hypocondriacal symptoms, and in great anguish spoke of the imminent Last Judgment. He took himself for a prince, a king, an emperor, Christ; his hallucinations (later represented in drawings) manifested visions of a prophet, a pope, the Antichrist, and the Spirit of God in the clouds. After having attempted suicide, he was interned, and subsequently manifested acute schizophrenic symptoms, marked by innumerable hallucinations.

> At first I saw a white spot in the cloud, very near by—the clouds all stood still—then the white spot withdrew and remained in the sky the whole time, like a board. On this board or screen or stage pictures followed one another like lightening, maybe 10,000 in half an hour, so that I could absorb the most important only with the greatest attention. The Lord himself appeared, the witch who created the world—in between there were worldly scenes: war pictures, parts of the earth, monuments, battle scenes from the Wars of Liberation, palaces, marvelous palaces, in short the beauties of the whole world—but all of these in supraearthy pictures. They were at least 20 meters high, could be seen clearly, and were almost colorless, like photographs; some were slightly colored. They were living figures which moved. At first I thought that they were not really alive; then they were transcended with ecstasy, the ecstasy was breathed into them. Finally it was like a movie. The meaning became immediately clear on first sight, even if one becomes conscious of the details only later while drawing them. The whole thing was very exciting and eerie. The pictures were manifestations of the last judgement. . . . They are revealed to me by God for the completion of the redemption.[9]

We find here the nightmare of a total cinema revealed in psychosis, where the libidinal thrusts of the return of the repressed counter the standardization and stereotypification typical of studio cinema production. Neter's hallucinations passed at the rate of about 10,000 per 30 minutes; that is, approximately 5½ images per second (or, as in the photomaton work described previously, at 3 frames per image)—certainly within the avant-garde capabilities of the silent-film speed of 16 frames per second.[10] How does this transformation or desublimation of theology into psychosis, and psychosis into cinema, arise? [figures 19 and 20]

What Peter Stallybrass and Allon White wrote of the transformation of carnival in *The Politics and Poetics of Transgression* may be claimed, *mutatis mutandis,* for the modern, bourgeois transformation of eschatological theology and apocalyptic visions:

> In the *Studies on Hysteria* many of the images and symbols which were once the focus of various pleasures in European carnival have become transformed into the morbid symptoms of private terror. . . . The demonization and the exclusion of the carnivalesque has to be related to the victorious emergence of specifically bourgeois practices and languages which reinflected and incorporated this material within a negative, individualist framework.[11]

Yet it is precisely the wrenching of such symbols, rites and symptoms from their cultural and theological contexts, and their inclusion in the realm of the psychopathological—precisely their violent, institutionalized secularization—that created the possibility of their recontextualization as extreme literary and artistic forms. What is at stake here is to establish precisely how the "other scene" of the unconscious, of the phantasmatic, of a certain imaginary, of madness, is discursively constituted and how the subject is constructed and situated within this linguistic and representational apparatus. Octave Mannoni, writing on the literary value of Daniel Paul Schreber's *Memoirs of My Nervous Illness,* suggested that psychiatric asylums are "prosthetic substitutes" for this other scene, and they thus constitute the topos of the social isolation of madness.[12] The asylum may thus be deemed a representational system of theater, one that is, traditionally, particularly closed—as closed as the psychic system of paranoia that breeds within its confines. This closure inaugurates a certain type of fantasy, a certain radical imagery, evident in the works of psychopathological art.

This was not lost on the Surrealists: both their advocacy of tapping the unconscious primary processes through the use of automatic writing and their iconography disclose a fascination with psychotic hallucinatory phenomena. In fact, Max Ernst carried Prinzhorn's book with him as a gift for Paul Eluard on his arrival in Paris in 1924. Ernst was particularly fascinated by this book, especially the case of Neter.

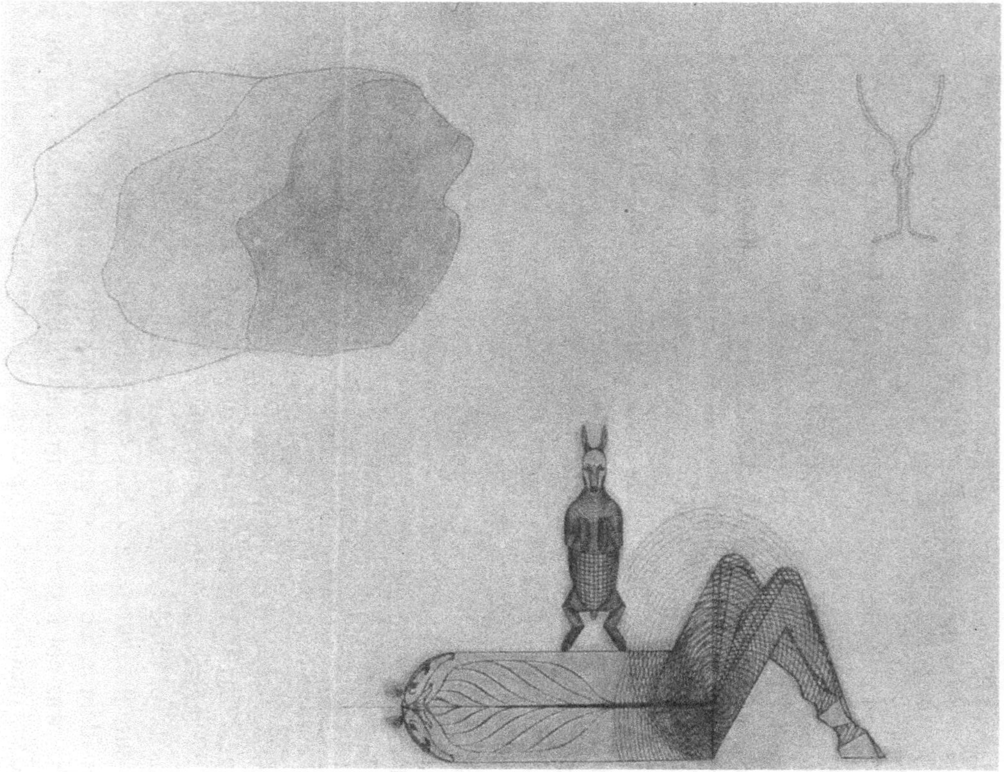

Figure 19. August Neter, "Axis of the World Rabbit," 1919 (photo I.L. Klinger, courtesy the Prinzhorn Collection, University of Heidelberg).

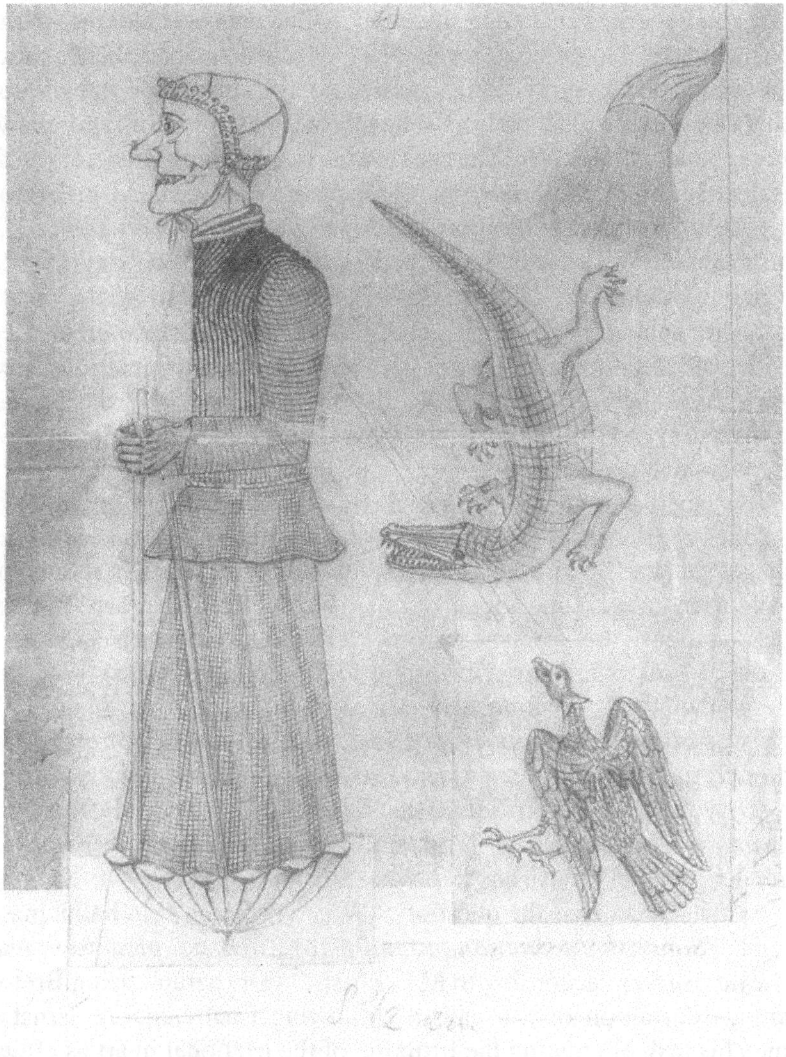

Figure 20. August Neter, "Witch," 1919 (photo I.L. Klinger, courtesy the Prinzhorn Collection, University of Heidelberg).

Indeed, probably the most cited example of the direct influence of the art of the insane on modern art is one of Ernst's works. When asked to design the cover of a special issue of the *Cahiers d'art* (1937) devoted to his own work, Ernst chose his 1931 collage entitled *Oedipe,* a transformation of Neter's drawing "The Marvellous Shepherd" into a Sphinx-headed figure holding the head of an animal (perhaps a lion). An "Oedipus" with a Sphinx's head conflates question and answer, enigma and solution. We find here what was to become one of the dialectical limits of the archetypical Surrealist quest, stated in Breton's preface to an Ernst exhibition of collage in 1920: "Who knows if, in this manner, we are not being prepared to escape one day from the principle of identity."[13] This sensibility was to prepare for the creation of Surrealism itself, with its dissociative and depersonalizing techniques of free association, automatic writing, chance operations, juxtaposition of incompatibles, hallucination, and especially the aesthetic valorization and simulation of madness. Ernst: "Identity will be convulsive or it will no longer be."[14]

In the issue of the *Cahiers d'Art* devoted to Ernst, his own text includes a celebration of Leonardo da Vinci's fascination with varied images that can be discovered in a splotch of paint left by a sponge on a wall or in cloud formations (human heads, animals, battle scenes, rocks, clouds, the sea, and so on).[15] These observations were at the origin of Ernst's invention of the *frottage* technique (1925)—a manner of spontaneously creating the equivalent of hypnagogic images. Yet this was no mere technique: for Ernst, it was a manner of expressing, through the creation of simulacra, his own visual obsessions. Inspired by a psychoaesthetic procedure that Salvador Dali would later term the *paranoic-critical method,* Ernst utilized this pictorial technique to, "render my soul monstrous."[16]

Ernst answered the question, "What is collage?" in hallucinatory terms: "*Simple hallucination,* according to Rimbaud, *placement under marine whiskey,* according to Max Ernst."[17] Or, paraphrasing Breton's famous definition of Surrealism (following Lautréamont), Ernst defined his task of creating the irruption of the irrational in art as effected by, "the fortuitous encounter to two distinct realities on an inappropriate plane."[18] This condition is met, a fortiori, in the work of collage. And yet, once the irrational irrupts into the artwork, it is transformed into a sort of manifest content of the psychic processes, thus overcoming a threshold of nonsense as it changes from passion to object.[19] Otherwise, our critical and theoretical processes would be useless. Or are they?

One quasi-cinematic work is emblematic of this quest. In his book, *Rêve d'une petite fille qui voulut entrer au Carmel* (Paris, 1930; *A Little Girl Dreams of Taking the Veil*), there is a collage of a Zoetrope from which the images of birds materialize, take flight, and escape, while a young girl finds herself in the very middle of the device, running in astonishment and perhaps fright.[20] This is the cinematic version of a primal aesthetic fantasy: the work of art come to life (the transformation and flight of the birds), coupled with life engulfed and transformed by the work of art (the presence of the girl in the apparatus). The kinship between collage juxtaposition and filmic montage is here allegorized in the very difference between the relative stasis of art and the dynamics of life.

We find the same allegory, utilizing a surrealizing collage within a cinematic animation, in Larry Jordan's film, *Patricia Gives Birth to a Dream by the Doorway* (1962–1964). (Jordan was the assistant of Joseph Cornell, who in turn was intimately associated with the Surrealists and was especially fond of Ernst's collage books.) In this film, we see Patricia, with her "dream" taking the form of a movie screen in the background, on which flickering images are projected. The climax of the film harkens back to the origins of cinema, in the very same sort of Zoetrope dreamed of by Ernst's little girl who took the veil: first, a bird leaves the screen to fly into the landscape surrounding it; then a flight of bees leaves the screen to swarm into the room past the girl; then a star falls into a lake (perhaps an allusion to *Revelation*, where after the opening of the seventh seal the star called Wormwood shot flaming from the sky and fell into the waters of the earth); and finally an egg takes flight. Yet this work is far from the apocalyptic or the mad: it is Surrealism reduced to its formal genius.

The masterpiece that combines collage, cinema, and the simulacrum of madness is Harry Smith's film *No. 12* (circa the late 1950s), also known as *Heaven and Earth Magic* or *The Magic Feature*. This animation is a filmic montage of collage (the images taken from old catalogues and books), in part inspired by Smith's own dream imagery, in part constructed by Surrealist automatic and chance techniques ("Exquisite Corpse"), and in part derived from his fascination with certain key psychopathological texts.[21] A synoptic description of Smith's film would be impossible, due to the emphatically disjunctive nature of the narrative. Consider his own description of one scene:

> Then there's a graveyard scene, when the dead are all raised again. What actually happens at the end of the film is everybody's put in a teacup, because all kinds of horrible monsters came out of the graveyard, like animals that folded into one another. Then everyone gets thrown in a teacup, which is made out of a head, and stirred up. This is the Trip to Heaven and the Return, then the Noah's Ark, then The Raising of the Dead, and finally the Stirring of Everyone in a Teacup.[22]

Compare the following:

> It seemed as if a broom were sweeping inside his chest and stomach; his skin had turned into fur; his bones and throat were petrified; in his stomach he had a tree trunk; his blood consisted of water, animals came out of his nose. He sees the devil in the shape of a column of fire perform dances in front of him; when he puts his hand on the table it is as though he touches the wood with the bones; poems about him appear in the newspaper; he is Antichrist, the genuine one; he must live forever, he could not die; he no longer has a heart, his soul was torn out. He explains the cracking of his knees as telephone calls by which the devil down below is always notified of his whereabouts.[23]

This is not a further description of *Heaven and Earth Magic;* rather, it is an account of August Neter's psychotic deliria. We know that the destruction of the ego in schizophrenia is psychically represented by the dismembered, fragmented, transformed, violated body. This delusional projection of the psychotic's body is then prey to a recombinatory system, where the body may be plugged into machines, abused by others, or controlled by God or the Devil. Jacques Lacan explained:

> This fragmented body . . . usually manifests itself in dreams when the movement of the analysis encounters a certain level of aggressive disintegration in the individual. It then appears in the form of disjointed limbs, or of those organs represented in exoscopy, growing wings and taking up arms for intestinal persecutions—the very same that the visionary Hieronymous Bosch has fixed, for all time, in painting their ascent from the fifteenth century to the imaginary zenith of modern man. But this form is even tangibly

> revealed at the organic level, in the lines of "fragilization" that define the anatomy of phantasy, as exhibited in the schizoid and spasmodic symptoms of hysteria.[24]

The symbolic reaggregation of body projections, of *disjecta membra*, corresponds with the psychic attempt at ego reintegration, contemporaneous with the attempt to reinstate object cathexes to fight against the anxiety found at the source of the illness. Victor Tausk, in his classic essay, "On the Origin of the Influencing Machine in Schizophrenia" (1918), explained that one of the principle effects of such paranoid "influencing machines" is that "It makes the patients see pictures. When this is the case, the machine is generally a magic lantern or cinematograph."[25]

Harry Smith confirmed the hallucinatory nature of *Heaven and Earth Magic* by asserting that it takes place in the fissure of Silvius, one of the folds of the brain; furthermore, its paranoid function as an influencing machine is revealed by his claim that, "My movies are made by God; I was just the medium for them."[26] Such statements seems to fall, as it were, into what might be termed the *antinomies of pure aesthetics*. We can never determine whether any given statement is dictated by the speaker or inspired by God; we can never determine whether any given statement is dictated by consciousness or the unconscious. This is precisely the gambit of Surrealism: although valorizing the dreamwork, psychotic hallucinations, automatic expression, hysterical delirium, and so forth, there can never be any guarantee of whether the surreal artwork is a "projection" of these psychic processes or merely an allegory of them. But this determination is of little import; what is critical to their project is the simultaneous representation and celebration of the new forms that arise from the unconscious *and* the new spectatorial positions made possible by these representations. For such works—as well as the works of Art Brut and Écrits Bruts championed by Dubuffet, or the Katatonenkunst polemicized by Arnulf Rainer—not only add to our modernist catalogue of disarticulated narratives and grotesque iconography; their manifest content, fascinating as it may be, indicates a deeper latent content, which always remains at a distance, yet always exerts its magnetic attraction, its psychic causality. But these works also imply new aesthetic principles. Now, art must also be considered according to its desublimatory limits, precisely those margins of culture that might simply be termed life itself, according to that rebel Surrealist

Artaud. It is perhaps the intuition of such an (anti)aesthetic position that led Artaud, in "Sorcellerie et cinéma" (1927), to write of a *"cinéma brut."*[27]

Might not the paranoid organization of the symbolic be the very condition of faith (especially so heretical a faith as that of Schreber, Wölfli, Neter, and Artaud)? Might not the oneiric organization of the symbolic be a precondition of magic (whether heavenly or earthly)? The abyss, the fundamental magma, of the shattered symbolic must be the place where we rediscover the strange coherence of a certain modernist art. For such surreal works as have been discussed here are evidence of the fractured manifestations of our souls, of our convulsive attempts to escape the principle of self-identity. Perhaps the only way for us to adequately approach these works is not through our aesthetic theories, but through the deliria that such art produces.

TWELVE

Edible Architecture, Cannibal Architecture

Beauty will be edible, or it
will no longer be.
—*Salvador Dali*

A miraculous gingerbread house in the middle of the forest, ornamented with cakes and tarts and windows formed of barleysugar. Two young children, Hansel and Gretel, abandoned by their parents, lost in the woods, ravaged by hunger, come upon this hallucinatory spectacle and partake of its delights. This wish fulfillment, this extreme oral gratification, temporarily assuaging the terror of being abandoned, in fact veils an ever-greater and more primal fear: that of being devoured. For the charming gingerbread house is but a lure, a trap, inhabited by a wicked old woman who captures the children and intends to eat them. The pleasure of eating dissimulates its opposite, the threat of being devoured, for the confectionary house hides its origin, the very oven that is to be the site of the childrens' destiny. A single location, where the edible dissimulates the cannibal, is simultaneously utopic and dystopic, revealing the antithetical sense of primal gustatory emotions. The architectural *heimlich* (homey) conceals its *unheimlich* (uncanny) mystery, its *arcanum arcanorum,* where the ultimate secret of life is revealed: death.[1] In such intermingled pleasure and anxiety we have established the antipodal limits of our subject. Yet, as we shall see, not all are as lucky as these two children who escape from their gastronomic, indeed gastrophobic or gastrophagic, fate.

Edible architecture; cannibal architecture—the origins and genesis of such monstrosities are a function of psychological projection, where unconscious impulses organize the perceptual gestalt. Consider

Leonardo da Vinci's fascination with the varied images that can be discovered in cloud formations or in a splotch of paint left by a sponge on a wall: human heads, animals, battle scenes, rocks, clouds, the sea, and so forth. Can we not discover in a distant landscape what appears to be a human head with gaping mouth, as objectified in scenes of hell painted by Bosch or Breughel, or in the double images of Salvador Dali? The rhetorical trope of catachresis, producing monstrosities, creates such disquieting iconographic figures as "to enter the mouth of a cave" or "to be devoured by the earth," or "to descend into the bowels of the earth." Although the oneiric, infantile representations of the home tend toward the stable and the regular, as Gaston Bachelard reminded us, representations of the earth are often conducive of a dynamic, chaotic, labyrinthine imagination.[2] These images often skirt the limits of the horrific, the grotesque, the buffonic. For example, in the Bomarzo gardens, north of Rome, Orsini established a series of fantastic garden follies. We find there a gigantic, howling face, created by Pyrrho Ligorio. This *Ogre* (1551) is over ten feet tall, such that we may cautiously enter through the mouth into its shadowy interior, to find the tongue formed by a picnic table, and the seats created by the teeth surrounding it. Here, the utopic and dystopic orders are reversed in relation to the gingerbread house: in Bomarzo, we are eaten, only to be invited to eat. Yet, as opposed to the marked symbolism of Grimm's fairy tale, the potentially dyspeptic, cannibalistic fantasy of Bomarzo in fact is highly theatrical and ultimately frivolous, as is the entirety of the space of the Italian Renaissance garden. Indeed, the form of the mouth as theater also exists in the other arts. Consider, for example, Maurice Sendak's stage design for the film version of that other disquieting, balletic fairy tale, Tchaikovsky's *The Nutcracker*.[3] The stage curtain is composed of a gigantic head of the Nutcracker himself; closing vertically, it devours all those on stage. Or, in an equally astounding and disquieting theatrical representation, there exists a drawing by the famed geneticist turned psychotic artist Eugène Gabritschevsky, which depicts a stage setting where the proscenium is composed of an open, toothed, menacing mouth.[4] We find in his art the poetic manifestations of the Darwinian imagination gone berserk, where scientific genetic illustration is transformed into the most extreme iconography of the grotesque. How are we to understand these ravenous, often demonic, doubles of ourselves?

The major theoretical, polemical, statement on edible architecture and cannibal architecture was written by Salvador Dali, *"De la beauté terrifiante et comestible de l'architecture modern style"* (On the Terrifying and Edible Beauty of Art Nouveau Architecture").[5] Dali explained that Art Nouveau (Modern Style) architecture is the first to be based on the oneiric manifestations of desire. This invention of an "hysterical sculpture" is derived from Art Nouveau's fascination with organic, rather than mechanical, forms. The paradigm of Art Nouveau architecture is based on the fluid "sculpting of reflections of crepescular clouds in water." These forms manifest the "hard undulations of *sculpted water* with a photographic concern for instantaneity." In fact, this notion explains the profound relations between Art Nouveau and the Baroque, which can be summed up in Jean Rousset's observation that a Baroque facade is the aquatic reflection of a Renaissance facade.[6] Dali described these effects: "an immense and insane multicolored and gleaming mosaic of pointillist iridescences from which emerge the forms of pouring water, the forms of stagnant water, the forms of glistening water, the forms of water grazed by the wind."[7]

These possibilities already existed, at least in the culinary creations of Carême, the greatest French chef of the nineteenth century, who was able to create the waves of the sea, waterfalls, rivers, and so forth by means of the subtle nuances of spun sugar.[8] Thus not only do our arts and our dreams provide us with architecture in the form of food; the history of gastronomy also exhibits creations where food is presented in the form of architecture. Yet that which in Dali's architectural imagination approaches the perverse manifestations of the sublime would, in fact, reach the extreme of the picturesque in Carême's hands. The epitome of the influence of architecture on gastronomy is undoubtedly to be found in Carême's pastry, where he created a landscape architecture based on the organic forms of nature that is truly, and not merely metaphorically, edible. Two of his books, *Le Pâtissier Parisien* and *Le Pâtissier Pittoresque,* contain numerous architectural drawings that are, in fact, projects for exceedingly elaborate desserts.[9] Carême, deemed the "Palladio of cooking," created gastronomic-architectural fantasies (sometimes over a meter tall) that encompassed the entire range of subjects and nations: pavillions, rotundas, temples, ruins, towers, belvederes, fortresses, waterfalls, fountains, country homes, thatched cottages, mills, hermitages; Italian, Turkish, Islamic,

Russian, Polish, Venetian, Chinese, Irish, Gallic, Egyptian. He even dreamed of a durabililty far beyond that of the average dessert: by means of confectioning his creations in a mixture of gum arabic, gum tragacanth, sugar, starch, and marble dust, his architectural desserts were able to last as long as six years. Consider, for example, his miniature trompe-l'oeil dessert representing a "grotto covered with moss," with the rocks constructed of small cakes glazed with different types of sugar (pink, caramelized, saffron) and coated with crystal sugar and chopped pistachios, then surrounded with meringue and vanilla cream, and crowned with a waterfall of silvered spun sugar.[10]

These fantasies could be seen as the frivolous doubles of Grimm's nightmarish gingerbread house, conceived in the same epoch. Today, such inventions are, alas, relegated to history. Contemporary gastronomic architecture is much more modest. For example at Lasserre, the renowned Parisian restaurant, each course arrives at the table accompanied by a small decorative spun sugar building; or, most modest of all, are the sugar-coated praline pebbles of the great confectioner Auer in Nice, pebbles that can be distinguished from those on the nearby beach only by means of taste. It is rather in the cinema, with its desire for scopophilic excess and verisimilitude, that this tradition has been, at least briefly and ironically, resuscitated. In Peter Greenaway's film, *The Belly of an Architect,* we witness a Roman feast in which the centerpiece consists of a culinary reproduction of one of the masterpieces of French revolutionary architecture: Etienne-Louis Boullée's *Cénataph à Newton*. This monument becomes an icon of the film and the architect's fate, a cinematic *vanitas* or memento mori. Like the oven in the gingerbread house, the mausoleum-cake reveals the intimate connection between food and death and effectively symbolizes the morbid personality and impending demise of the architect himself. (And we might note that Carême's Romantic miniature picturesque was in part a tangential reaction to Boullée's Rationalist monumental sublime.)

Dali understood the deepest psychological implications of such efforts, exemplified for him by the commonplace, yet delirious, comparison of Art Nouveau architecture with pastry. Such a homology affords us the unheard of possibility of eating the objects of our architectural desire. This return to a more primal, since edible, beauty evinces Dali's realization that, "Erotic desire is the ruin of intellectualist aesthetics"—such that architecture is oneiric and symbolic before it is pragmatic. Following the surrealist ontology and epistemology of transforming the forms of the world according to the lineaments of our desires, these gustatory passions were not lost on Dali's own work. His iconography, governed by the double imagery of his paranoic-critical method, abounds in mountains, monuments, and buildings in the form of melting cheese (e.g., *La naissance des désirs liquides* (1932)); faces which are part of the landscape (e.g., *Apparition of a Face and a Fruit Dish on a Beach* (1938)); and skulls transplanted in the scenery, transforming the landscape into a veritable *vanitas,* literally a *nature morte,* (e.g., *Tête de mort atmosphérique sodomisant un piano à queue* (1934)).

The connections between pleasure and nostalgia, mortality and destiny, history and monumentality are central to the pictorial genre of *vanitas,* of which the *still life* or *nature morte* is a subcategory often revealing the utmost gastronomic splendor. The pleasures of life, intense yet transitory, are represented by a network of symbols: tables overflowing with rare foods, adorned with intricate silverwork, fine crystal, brilliant floral bouquets.[11] Yet such sensual exhiliration is tempered by the threat of melancholy. The work of Time the destroyer is everywhere apparent: the last grains of sand are about to drop in an hourglass; the fruit is just slightly too ripe and threatened by an insect; a bubble—perhaps reflecting the very image of the artist, our double—is about to burst.

Yet the threat to a portrayed figure can take a decidedly more culinary form. The tradition of the still life, in its most perverse manifestations, occasionally takes on a distinctly cannibalistic turn. Most astounding in this regard are Giuseppe Arcimboldo's composite portraits, such as *The Four Seasons* (1573), a strange variation on the classic iconography of the ages of man, where the heads are composed of flowers (Spring), fruits and vegetables (Summer and Autumn), and leaves and branches (Winter); his portrait of *The Cook* (circa 1570), whose head is composed of animals on a platter, ready to be served; or *The Vegetable Gardener* (circa 1590), an image consisting of assorted vegetables in a bowl that, when turned upside down, reveals a man's head.[12] Other manifestations, by other artists, also exist, and that this passion should be displayed in pastry design is not surprising. Casanova recounted the story of a fabulous dinner he had created in Cologne. The finale was a cake on which were represented the portraits of all the sovereigns of Europe. Casanova's passion for royalty was symbolically manifested in this attempt at complete devoration. As

Chantal Thomas explained: "A superb *potlach.* They risked indigestion, they gorged themselves with, they feasted upon, kings. They stuffed their pockets with them. Upon their return, they found bits of Louis XV or of Catherine stuck to the lining of their clothes, their fingers were sticky with them, they distractedly nibbled on them."[13] Symbolic overcompensation or childish reaction? As we say of an adorable child: "I could eat him up!" Needless to say, as Kleinian psychoanalysis teaches us, the dynamics of love and hate are played out through the mechanics of devoration and expulsion, incorporation and expropriation.

This dialectic of "dead life" *(nature morte)* is played out in two related works by Marcel Duchamp: *Torture-morte* (1959), consisting of a plaster foot covered with flies; and *Sculpture-morte* (1959), a head à la Arcimboldo composed of marzipan vegetables and an insect, one of the very rare *trompe l'oeil* artworks that can actually be eaten. In these two works, the symbolism of *vanitas* is divided into its component parts: as the fly on *Sculpture-morte* (a perverse still life) symbolically warns us of our own destiny, the flies on *Torture-morte* (a morbid antiportrait) reveal the ultimate limit of our fate. Duchamp: "Men are mortal, pictures too."[14]

But the drama may be reversed: architectural phantasmagoria can also be projected as a utopian, life-giving delicacy. In James Joyce's *Ulysses,* Leopold Bloom, who "ate with relish the inner organs of beasts and fowls" and whose famous breakfast consisted of fried kidneys, imagines at one point that a new era is at hand, where "ye shall ere long enter into the golden city which is to be, the new Bloomusalem in the Nova Hibernia of the future." The description that follows obeys classic dream logic, incorporating the residues of quotidian events, with their gastric and gastronomic homologues, into the dreamwork: "Thirtytwo workmen wearing rosettes, from all the counties of Ireland, under the guidance of Derwan the builder, construct the new Bloomusalem. It is a colossal ediface, with crystal roof, built in the shape of a huge pork kidney, containing forty thousand rooms."[15] Such an architectural design obeys the rare, surreal, organic laws foreshadowing the later work of Frederick Kiesler, whose model for the *Endless House* (1959) resembles Boschian plant husks or transected intestinal parts, who designed a house in the form of a tooth (1947), and whose *Grotto for Meditation* (1963) was conceived in the form of a fish.[16] An equally grotesque image is Victor Hugo's drawing, *L'intestin de Léviathan,* which illustrates the following passage from his *Les misérables* (Part 5): "PARIS! What are its intestines? The sewers . . . " Or quite differently, the surreal and the neoclassic occasionally combine in post-modern paradox: witness the project by Sacha Sosno, of the École de Nice, consisting of a building in the form of a head, whose upper part is obliterated by a square block. Yet Sosno's perturbed neoclassicism does not quite reach the disquieting limits that his project announces and that is foreshadowed by the following thought of Victor Hugo: "The house, like man, can become a skeleton."[17]

Unlike the gingerbread house, here edible architecture and cannibal architecture find their common ground in the aesthetic sublimation of our most primal desires and fears. But what happens when the course of history transforms these passions and fears into prodigious instantiations of universal destiny? Dali's exegesis of the desublimated oneiric beauty of liquid architecture also reveals what he terms, "the apparition of the cannibal imperialism of the Modern Style." This enunciation of what we may term the *anxiety of architecture* was written in 1933: "cannibal imperialism" was already far more than just a psychoaesthetic metaphor. It was on the verge of becoming an historical nightmare, where the sheer terror and dread at the source of the aesthetic sublime came to the fore, placing us on the edge of, indeed within, the abyss. For the tale of the gingerbread house foreshadows its demonic, hyperbolic double: the ovens of Auschwitz.

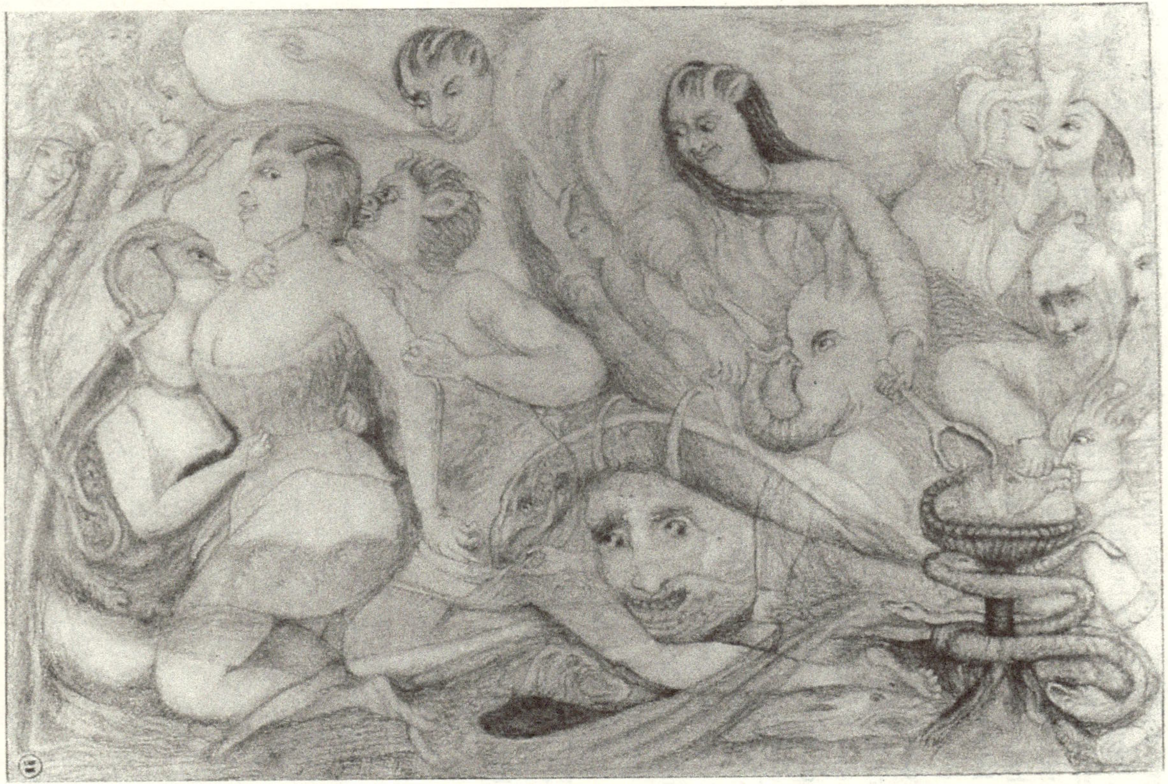

Figure 21. Comte de Tromelin, “Women and Monsters,” n.d. (photo courtesy the Collection de l’Art Brut, Lausanne).

NOTES

INTRODUCTION

1. Arthur Rimbaud, "Letter to Paul Demeny" (15 May 1871) in *Illuminations,* trans. Louise Varèse (New York: New Directions, 1957), p. xxx.
2. Jean Dubuffet, "Art Brut in Preference to the Cultural Arts" [1949], trans. Allen S. Weiss and Paul Foss, in *Art Brut: Madness and Marginalia,*" ed. Allen S. Weiss; a special issue of *Art & Text* 27 (1988), p. 33.
3. Jean Dubuffet, "Notes," in *Dubuffet: Culture et subversion, L'ARC #35* (1968), p. 84. See also, "L'Art Brut" [1959], in Jean Dubuffet, *Prospectus et tous écrits suivants,* Vol. #1 (Paris: Gallimard, 1967), p. 515.

CHAPTER 1. THE PRIMACY OF MATTER

1. André Breton, *Nadja* [1928], trans. Richard Howard (New York: Grove Press, 1960), p. 52.
2. André Breton, *L'amour fou* [1937] (Paris: Gallimard, 1982), p. 42.
3. Jean Dubuffet, "Saint-Ouen—Le Marché," *Prospectus et tous écrits suivants,* vol. 1, p. 108; hereafter *Prospectus.*
4. Jean Dubuffet, Letter to Jacques Berne (15 May 1949), *Prospectus,* vol. 2, pp. 433–434.
5. Jean Dubuffet, Letter to Gaston Chaissac (24 June 1947), *Prospectus,* vol. 1, p. 466.
6. Paul Robert, *Le Petit Robert: Dictionnaire de la langue française* (Paris: Société du Nouveau Littré, 1972), p. 1056.
7. On the problematic of sublimation and desublimation in Surrealism, see my, "Between the Sign of the Scorpion and the Sign of the Cross: *L'Age d'or,*" in Allen S. Weiss, *The Aesthetics of Excess* (Albany: State University of New York Press, 1989).
8. See the catalogue of L'Aracine, *L'Aracine: Art Brut* (1988), available at the museum at Neuilly-sur-Marne, p. 88.
9. Michel Thévoz, *Dubuffet* (Geneva: Skira, 1986), p. 41.
10. Dubuffet and Bataille probably met in 1922 at the rue Blomet studio of André Masson, which they both frequented. This meeting place was the

rendezvous of many writers and artists—including Artaud, Leiris, and Limbour—who were to later align themselves against Breton and mainstream Surrealism.

11. George Bataille, "Formless" in *Visions of Excess,* trans. Allan Stoekl (Minneapolis: University of Minnesota Press, 1985), p. 31.
12. Jean Dubuffet, Letter to Michel Tapié (21 December 1952), *Prospectus,* vol. 2, p. 308.
13. Jean Dubuffet, "Notes pour les fins-lettrés," *Prospectus,* vol. 1, p. 54.
14. This in fact predates John Cage's first attempts at chance operations in art by several years.
15. Jean Dubuffet, Letter to André Pieyre de Mandiargues (29 May 1959), *Prospectus,* vol. 1, p. 468.
16. Michel Nedjar, "I Am Tied to the Threads of the World," trans. Roger Cardinal, *Art & Text* 27 (1988): 53–54.
17. Ibid., pp. 55–56.
18. Ibid., p. 54.
19. Ibid., p. 55 (augmented translation).
20. Cited in an interview of Michel Nedjar (January 1985), available only in English translation by Corinne Cantrill; republished in *Art Brut: Madness and Marginalia,* p. 57.
21. Michel Nedjar, "L'Art des transformations," *Alternes,* 1, 1980, p. 21.
22. Jean Dubuffet, "L'Auteur répond a quelques objections" [1946], *Prospectus,* vol. 2, p. 66.
23. Michel Thévoz, *Dubuffet,* p. 36.
24. Jean Dubuffet, "Empreintes," *Prospectus,* vol. 2, pp. 148–149.
25. Gaston Bachelard, *La terre et les rêveries de la volonté* (Paris: José Corti, 1947), p. 96.
26. Maurice Merleau-Ponty, *Phenomenology of Perception,* trans. Colin Smith (London: Routledge & Kegan Paul, 1970), p. 237.

CHAPTER 2. IN THE DEVIL'S KITCHEN

1. Umberto Eco., "An *Ars Oblivionalis?* Forget It!" *PMLA* 103, no. 3 (1981): 255. This section of my text is indebted to Eco's article.
2. Ibid., p. 257.
3. Frances A. Yates, *The Art of Memory* (Chicago: University of Chicago Press, 1966), pp. 105–128, passim. My work is deeply indebted to this classic text on the art of memory. An excellent phenomenological study on the topic is Edward S. Casey, *Remembering* (Bloomington and Indianapolis: Indiana University Press, 1987).

4. Yates, ibid., pp. 50–81, passim. Yates made the fascinating suggestion that Dante's *Inferno* may thus be in part understood as a mnemonic system for remembering the torments of Hell and that many pictorial artworks of the Renaissance were at least in part modeled on the iconic structures of memory systems.
5. Cited in Eco, "An *Ars Oblivionalis?*" p. 257.
6. Ambroise Paré, *On Monsters and Marvels*, trans. Janis L. Pallister (Chicago: University of Chicago Press, 1982), pp. 3–4. See also, Claude Kappler, *Monstres, démons et merveilles à la fin du Moyen Age* (Paris: Payot, 1980).
7. For a typology of monsters, see Kappler, ibid., pp. 115–183, passim; see also Gilbert Lascaux, *Le monstre dans l'art occidental* (Paris: Klincksieck, 1973), pp. 115–175, passim.
8. Cited in Yates, *Art of Memory*, p. 10.
9. Michel Nedjar, "I Am Tied to the Threads of the World," p. 57.
10. Ibid., pp. 53–59, passim.
11. Ibid., pp. 56–57.
12. Roger Cardinal, "Within Us These Traces," *Art & Text* 27 (1988): 49.
13. Bruno Schulz, "Tailors' Dummies," *The Street of Crocodiles*, trans. Celina Wieniewska (New York: Penguin, 1977), pp. 61–62.
14. Eco, "An *Ars Oblivionalis?*" p. 259.
15. Ibid., pp. 259–260. We might consider in this repect Borges's tale, "Funes the Memorious," trans. James E. Irby, *Labyrinths* (New York: New Directions, 1964), whose protagonist has totally perfect recall, to the point where conceptualization was impossible for him, because the idea of, for example, "leaf," entailed the recall of every view of every leaf that he ever saw. This fantasy brings to mind Nietzsche's own critique of conceptuality in "On Truth and Lie in an Extra-Moral Sense," where he showed, utilizing the same concept of "leaf," that every concept originates in equating what is in fact unequal.
16. Yates, *Art of Memory*, pp. 231–242, passim.
17. Cited in Philippe Ariès, *The Hour of Our Death*, trans. Helen Weaver (New York: Alfred A. Knopf, 1981), p. 513. This majestic work is one of our richest sources on the history and historiography of death.
18. Ibid., p. 516.
19. This study might serve as the basis for a reinterpretation of what are perhaps the oldest extant examples of the art of the mentally ill, several drawings by the fourteenth century Italian cleric Opicinus de Canistris, discussed by Ernst Kris in "A Psychotic Artist of the Middle Ages," in *Psychoanalytic Explorations in Art* (New York: International Universities Press, 1952), pp. 118–127. Kris notes that these images are unlike anything else in Medieval art. This is true in regard to art per se, but he fails to

make the connection between their formal characteristics and those of memory theaters. In fact, these drawings bear an uncanny resemblance to Renaissance memory theaters, which were to a great extent based upon more rudimentary Medieval models and theories. Recognition of this connection would, in fact, reinforce the psychological implications of Kris' interpretation of Canistris, which deals with the problematic of psychotic repression and forgetting.

CHAPTER 3. FIGURATIONS AND DISFIGURATIONS

1. On the history and nature of physiognomy, see Jurgis Baltrušaitis, "Physiognomie animale," *Aberrations* (Paris: Flammarion, 1983), pp. 8–53; Jean-Jacques Courtine and Claudine Haroche, *Histoire du visage* (Paris: Rivages, 1988); Patrizia Magli, "The Face and the Soul," *Zone* 4 (1989): 86–127, *Fragments for a History of the Human Body*, Part Two.
2. Emmanuel Levinas, "Meaning and Sense," *Collected Philosophical Papers,* trans. Alphonso Lingis (Dordrecht: Martinus Nijhoff, 1987); pp. 95–96.
3. We should remember that film and theater acting produces conventionalized, i.e., symbolic, facial expressions. This should not be mistaken for quotidian expressiveness. Also, the meaning of a given expression or gesture is most certainly culturally determined and may vary from culture to culture.
4. On Tschirtner's drawings, see Leo Navratil, *Über schizophrenie und die Federzeichnungen des Patienten O.T.* (Verlag Gmbh & Co. KG): the French edition of this work is *Schizophrénie et art,* trans. Evelyne Sznycer, (Brussels: Éditions Complexe, 1978).
5. Although premodern myths contain a multitude of such hybrids, created from the inmixing of humans and *animals,* we should note that the rise of the modern mechanical age saw a new type of "monstrosity"—and occasionally beauty—created from the combination of humans and *machines*. This novel paradigm is at the center of the genre of "science fiction." For a discussion of the origins of this possibility, see Annette Michelson, "On the Eve of the Future: The Reasonable Facsimile and the Philosophical Toy," *October* 29 (1984): 2–20.
6. On Michel Nedjar's dolls, see Roger Cardinal, "Within Us These Traces"; and Michel Nedjar, "I Am Tied to the Threads of the World."
7. Claude Lévi-Strauss, *The Way of the Masks,* trans. Sylvia Modelski (Seattle: University of Washington Press, 1982), p. 120.

8. On prohibition, transgression, and the mythic institution of symbolic systems, see Allen S. Weiss, "Possession Trance and Dramatic Perversity," *The Aesthetics of Excess*, pp. 3–11.
9. The hermeneutic context of the artwork may be determined according to three major intertwined rubrics: *semiologically* in the context of other artwork (i.e., as sign); *biographically* in the context of the artist's life (i.e., as symptom); and *sociologically* in the context of cultural systems (i.e., as object, whether sacred or profane, mythical or economic). The relative importance of each of these categories varies from work to work.
10. Daniel Paul Schreber, *Memoirs of My Nervous Illness*, trans. Ida Macalpine and Richard A. Hunter (Cambridge, Mass.: Harvard University Press, 1988); for detailed studies of this case, see *Psychosis and Sexual Identity: Toward a Post-Analytic View of the Schreber Case*, ed. David B. Allison, Prado de Oliveira, Mark S. Roberts, Allen S. Weiss (Albany: State University of New York Press, 1988).
11. George Bataille, "Eye," *Visions of Excess*, trans. Allan Stoekl (Minneapolis: Minnesota University Press, 1985), p. 17.
12. André Breton, *Nadja*, p. 89.
13. Guy Rosolato, "Recension du corps," *Élements de l'interprétation* (Paris: Gallimard, 1985), pp. 239–240.
14. Lévi-Strauss, *Way of the Masks*, p. 144.
15. See, *L'Art Brut*, Fascicule 12: *Gugging* (Lausanne: Collection de l'Art Brut, 1983).
16. Compare the works of Arnulf Rainer. See the catalogue to the 1989 retrospective at the Guggenheim Museum, curated by Rudi Fuchs.
17. Hans Prinzhorn, *Artistry of the Mentally Ill*, pp. 40–44, 231–234.

CHAPTER 4. THE NEW DISFIGURATION

1. Gilles Deleuze, *Francis Bacon: Logique de la sensation*, Vol. 1 (Paris: Éditions de la différence, 1981), p. 80.
2. A recent exhibition of interest in this regard is *Figurative Inventions*, at the Museum of Modern Art (New York, 1990), a show of seventy-five Expressionist prints from Northern Europe.
3. Gregory Whitehead, "The Forensic Theater: Memory Plays for the Post-Mortem Condition," *Performing Arts Journal* 35–36 (1990). Whitehead's radiophonic creations, especially *Display Wounds* and *Disorder Speech*, are concerned with these issues.
4. See, Emmanuel Levinas and Françoise Armengaud, "On Obliteration," *Art & Text* 33 (1989); the full text of this interview was published as *De*

l'oblitération (Paris: Éditions de la différence, 1990). See also the catalogue to the show *Sosno Sculptures,* at the Tampa (Florida) Museum of Art, 1989.

5. We are reminded of this lineage once again in the catalogue essay by Mildred Glimcher accompanying the Fall 1990 show at the Pace Gallery in New York, *de Kooning/Dubuffet: The Women*.
6. David Sylvester, *Interviews with Francis Bacon* (London: Thames & Hudson, 1975), p. 112. See the catalogue of the retrospective Bacon exhibition at the Museum of Modern Art (New York), 1990.
7. We find a fascinating, quasi-scientific version of this phenomenon in the work of Eugéne Gabritschevsky, a famed Russian geneticist who went mad in 1929 and spent the rest of his life in psychiatric hospitals, where he created thousands of drawings, many of which are phantasmatic versions of his earlier scientific research—mutations of mutations. See the catalogue *Donations Daniel Cordier* (Paris: Centre Georges Pompidou, 1989).
8. Deleuze, *Francis Bacon,* p. 83.
9. Sylvester, *Interviews with Francis Bacon,* p. 23.
10. See Roger Cardinal, "Michel Nedjar" *L'Art Brut*" *L'Art Brut* (Lausanne: Collection de l'Art Brut, 1990). Nedjar's dolls can be seen in the collections at the Centre Georges Pompidou (Donations Cordier); La Collection de l'Art Brut (Lausanne); and L'Aracine (Neuilly-sur-Marne, near Paris). In Autumn 1990, his drawings were exhibited at Bill Bace Gallery (New York), Galerie Susanne Zander (Cologne), Alpha Cubic Gallery (Tokyo), Schloss Ebenrain (Sissach, Switzerland), and in the exhibition *Portraits From the Outside,* Parsons School of Design Gallery (New York).
11. Michel Nedjar, "Of What Does the Spider Dream?" *Portraits From the Outside,* ed S. Carr, B. Farber, S. Farber, A. S. Weiss (New York: Parsons School of Design, 1990), p. 87; reprinted in *Sulfur* 27 (1990).
12. Ralph Merrifield, *The Archaeology of Ritual and Magic* (New York: New Amsterdam Press, 1987), p. 190.

CHAPTER 5. OUTSIDE IN

1. It is not without irony that one of the works exhibited at La Villette is Cildo Meireles's *How to Build Cathedrals . . .*, which consists in part of 2,000 bovine tibia.
2. Jean-Hubert Martin, Preface to the catalogue *Les Magiciens de la Terre* (Paris: Centre Georges Pompidou, 1989), p. 11.

3. See, for example, *The Arcimboldo Effect* (New York: Abbeville, 1987).
4. Eric Michaels, *For a Cultural Future* (Melbourne: Artspace, 1987); pp. 39–57, passim.
5. We might remember that Nietzsche, especially in *Thus Spoke Zarathustra,* established a mythopoeic symbolism of the earth in opposition to the Western metaphysical tradition.
6. On the cultural specificity of shamanism, trance, and so forth, see Gilbert Rouget, *Music and Trance* (Chicago: University of Chicago Press, 1985); Felicitas D. Goodman, *How About Demons?* (Bloomington: Indiana University Press, 1988); Tobie Nathan, *Le sperme du diable* (Parus: PUF, 1988).
7. Homi Bhabha, "Hybridité, hétérogénéité et culture contemporaine," in *Les Magiciens de la Terre,* p. 27.

CHAPTER 6. A NEW ANXIETY OF INFLUENCE

1. Michel Thévoz, *Dubuffet;* all page references will follow citations in parenthesis.
2. We might note that Dubuffet had already suffered this hermeneutic fate in the writings of his major interpretor, the philosopher Max Loreau. Especially in his *Jean Dubuffet: Stratégie de la création* (Paris: Gallimard, 1973), Loreau presented a phenomenological reading of Dubuffet and the creative act, which actively eschewed all art historical—and indeed all historical!—considerations. Note that the phenomenological theorization of the ontological primary of the gesture (especially in the work of Maurice Merleau-Ponty) need not necessarily lead to this interpretive dead end.
3. Maurice Merleau-Ponty, *The Visible and the Invisible,* trans. Alphonso Lingis (Evanston, Ill.: Northwestern University Press, 1968), p. 125.
4. Fred Licht and Thomas Messer, *Jean Dubuffet & Art Brut* (Venice: The Peggy Guggenheim Collection, 1986), p. 7. Page numbers of all further references to this work will appear in parentheses within the text.
5. As early as 1922, in his *Artistry of the Mentally Ill,* Hans Prinzhorn argued that not only is there a deep cultural influence in certain artworks of the mentally ill, but also that many of the most interesting works of symbolic intent are precisely those where there is "a combat between instincts and cultural forces."
6. Michel Thévoz, *Art Brut,* trans. James Emmons (New York: Rizzoli/Skira, 1976), p. 9.

7. Another recent exhibition dealing more broadly with these issues was *Open Mind (Gesloten Circuits)* [Open Mind (Closed Circuits)], organized in 1990 by Jan Hoët (later director of the Documenta at Kassel) in Ghent, Belgium. Here, the art of the mentally ill, thirty works by Wölfli, as well as numerous others by relatively unknown Belgian patients, was placed in diametrical opposition to the art of the classic academy, with works by such artists as Van Gogh, Magritte, Borofsky, Weiner, Masson, Pollock, Twombly, Picabia, Rops, and Ensor, serving as the middle ground between the two latter poles or categories.
8. Arnulf Rainer, "Soliloquies" (1971), in *Arnulf Rainer,* the catalogue to the 1989 exhibition at the Solomon R. Guggenheim Museum in New York, curated by R.H. Fuchs, p. 36.
9. Cited in Franz Dahlem, "The Great Arch," *Arnulf Rainer,* ibid., p. 32. Note that this citation is translated differently in Rainer's essay "Face Farces," also included in the catalogue; p. 39. "I am only touched by calligraphic marks and the autistic theater of catatonics, a kind of art without pseudosocial wrapping."
10. "Katatonenkunst," *Manuskripte* (Graz, 1969); "Euthanasie der Kunst," *Neues Forum* (Vienna, 1969); "Die 13. Muse oder Wahsinn eine Kunstart," *Jahrbuch Protokolle* (Vienna, 1970); "Schön und Wahn," *Jahrbuch Protokolle* (Vienna, 1970); "Was aber ist Johann Hauser?" *Jahrbuch Protokolle* (Vienna, 1979). None of these articles was translated for the catalogue.
11. Arnulf Rainer, "Lamentation" (1982–83), *Arnulf Rainer,* p. 52.

CHAPTER 7. ART THERAPY, OUTREACH, ART BRUT

1. John MacGregor, *The Discovery of the Art of the Insane* (Princeton, N.J.: Princeton University Press, 1989), p. 311.
2. Cited in *European Outsiders* (New York: Rosa Esman Gallery, 1986), p. 135.
3. John MacGregor, "Marginal Outsiders: On the Edge of the Edge," in *Portraits from the Outside: Figurative Expression in Outsider Art,* p. 16.
4. Ibid., p. 12.
5. See Jean Dubuffet, "Honneur aux valeurs sauvages" [1951], in *Prospectus et tous écrits suivants,* vol. 1, pp. 203–224; and his letter to Dr. Volmat dated 28 December 1952, in ibid., p. 512.
6. Michel Thévoz and Allen S. Weiss, "Art Brut Today," in *Portraits From the Outside,* p. 19.
7. At the time of publication of this volume, the HAI policy prohibiting the sale of works of their artist-patients is apparently being reviewed.

CHAPTER 8. ÉCRITS BRUT

1. Antonin Artaud, "Artaud the Yoyo," trans. Clayton Eshelman, *Conductors of the Pit* (New York: Paragon House, 1988), pp. 148–149.
2. Friedrich Nietzsche, "On Truth and Lie in an Extra-Moral Sense," *The Portable Nietzsche,* trans. Walter Kaufman (New York: Viking Press, 1968), p. 46.
3. See Michel Thévoz, *Le langage de la rupture* (Paris: Presses Universitaires de France, 1978); Note that I have chosen to use the terms *mad, insane, mentally ill, schizophrenic, psychotic,* and *paranoid,* according to the usage demanded by the varying contexts of my discussion, rather than make an ideological statement by choosing to use a single term throughout. Nevertheless, the history and ideologies determining such usages demands a thorough study, which is beyond the scope of this text.
4. Jean Dubuffet, "Un grand salut très différent au Martelandre," in *Écrits bruts,* ed. Michel Thévoz (Paris: Presses Universitares de France, 1979), p. 231.
5. Jean Dubuffet, "Gaston le zoologue," *Prospectus et tous écrits suivants,* vol. 1 (Paris: Gallimard, 1967), p. 325.
6. See the "Pièces littéraires" Dubuffet's *Prospectus,* vol. 1; for example, "Ler dla canpane," "Anvouaiaje," and "Labonfam abeber." An excellent reading of these works is Michel Thévoz, "Dubuffet le casseur de noix," *Détournement d'écriture* (Paris: Minuit, 1989). My only reservation about his reading is the underestimation of, indeed refusal to admit, the influence of those écrits bruts that Dubuffet discovered in his own literary production. For a contemporary example of Artaud's influence, see also the literary, theatrical, and critical work of Valère Novarina, especially *Le drame de la vie, Le discours aux animaux, Vous qui habitez le temps,* and his essays in *Le théâtre des paroles* (all published in Paris by P.O.L.).
7. Bobon and Thévoz are cited by André Blavier, in *Les fous littéraires* (Paris: Éditions Henri Veyrier, 1982), pp 114–115. This book is a vast compendium of works by what Blavier terms *les fous littéraires.* Although not strictly speaking equivalent to the notion of écrits bruts (works that by definition were never intended for publication by their authors), Blavier's work in many ways supplements that of Dubuffet and Thévoz by revealing a category of writing that radically surpasses, and undermines, quotidian expression by its "madness."
8. Cited in *Adolf Wölfli,* ed. Elka Spoerri and Jürgen Glaesemer (Bern: The Adolf Wölfli Foundation, 1976), p. 111.
9. On Schreber, see *Psychosis and Sexual Identity: Toward a Post-Analytic View of the Schreber Case.* See also a Monique Plaza, *Écriture et folie*

(Paris: Presses Universitaires de France, 1986). Freud's text on Schreber is "Psychoanalytical Notes upon an Autobiographical Account of a Case of Paranoia (Dementia Paranoides)" [1911], in *Three Case Histories* (New York: Collier Books, 1973).

10. Octave Mannoni, "Writing and Madness," *Psychosis and Sexual Identity*, pp. 44 and 58.
11. Ibid.
12. Jean Dubuffet, "Art Brut Preferred to the Cultural Arts," trans. Paul Foss and Allen S. Weiss, *Art Brut: Madness and Marginalia*, p. 33.
13. Cited in Blavier, *Les fous littéraires*, p. 20, note 18.
14. Antonin Artaud, "Position de la chair," *Oeuvres Complètes* (Paris: Gallimard, 1976), p. 51. For an analysis of voice and body in Artaud, see Allen S. Weiss, "K." *A+T [Art & Text]* 37 (1990), pp. 56–59. For a more general account of this problematic, see Michel Pierssens, *The Power of Babel: A Study of Logophilia*, tr. Carl R. Lovitt (London: Routledge & Kegan Paul, 1980).

CHAPTER 9. MUSIC AND MADNESS

1. Louis Wolfson, *Le Schizo et les langues* (Paris: Gallimard, 1970). All citations from this book will be followed by the page number in parenthesis. See Chantal Thomas, "The War Against the Mother Tongue," *A+T (Art & Text)* 37 (1990), pp. 63–65.
2. Published in Paris in 1984 by Navarin Éditeur.
3. For a detailed study, see Walter Morgenthaler, *Adolf Wölfli [L'Art Brut,* Fascicule 2; Paris, 1964]. Most of my information on Wölfli is indebted to this text. Other major sources of information are *Adolf Wölfli*, the catalogue of the Wölfli Foundation in Berne, edited by Elka Spoerri and Jürgen Glaesemer (Bern: Museum of Fine Arts, 1976); *The Other Side of the Moon: The World of Adolf Wölfli*, edited by Elsa Longhauser and Elka Spoerri for the exhibition of the Goldie Paley Gallery of the Moore College of Art in Philadelphia, 1988. These works should be consulted for details of Wölfli's biography and art, a task far beyond the limited scope of this article.

   For a study of music and musication in the work of Artaud see Allen S. Weiss, "Psychopompomania," in *Art Brut: Madness and Marginalia*, reprinted in Weiss, *The Aesthetics of Excess*.
4. Daniel Paul Schreber, *Memoirs of My Nervous Illness* [1903], trans. Ida Macalpine and Richard A. Hunter (London: Wm Dawson and Sons, 1955), p. 176.

5. For a detailed account of the idiosyncrasies and the limits of the legibility of Wölfli's musical notation, see Peter Streiff and Kjell Keller, "Adolf Wölfli, Composer," in the catalogue *Adolf Wölfli* (Bern: Adolf Wölfli Foundation at the Museum of Fine Arts of Berne, 1976). See also *Adolf Wölfli: Dessinateur-Compositeur*, eds. Geneviève Roulin, Elka Spoerri, Michel Thévoz (Lausanne: L'Age d'Homme, 1991).
6. Cited in Elsbeth Pulver, "Signed: Adolf Wölfli, a Victim of Misfortune; Language Structure in Adolf Wölfli's Written Work," in Spoerri and Glaesemer, *Adolf Wölfli*, p. 78.

CHAPTER 10. RADIOPHONIC ART

1. Rabelais, *Pantagruel*, Book IV, Chs. LV and LVI, trans. Burton Raffel (New York: Norton, 1990).
2. Valère Novarina, "Chaos," *Le Théâtre de paroles* (Paris: P.O.L., 1989), p. 154.
3. "Lettre aux acteurs," in ibid., p. 17.
4. Ibid., p. 9.
5. The possibilities of such intersubjective, or rather intercorporeal exchange through recording techniques are developed in William Burroughs' *The Ticket That Exploded* (New York: Grove Weidenfeld, 1987), pp. 50–51: "The realization that something as familiar to you as the movement of your intestines the sound of your breathing the beating of your heart is also alien and hostile does make one feel a bit insecure at first. Remember that you can separate yourself from the 'Other Half' from the word. The word is spliced in with the sound of your intestines and breathing with the beating of your heart. The first step is to record the sounds of your body and start splicing them in yourself. Splice in your body sounds with the body sounds of your best friend and see how familiar he gets. Splice your body sounds in with air hammers. Blast jolt vibrate the 'Other Half' right out into the street. Splice your body sounds in with anybody or anything. Start a tapeworm club and exchange body sound tapes. Feel right out into your nabor's intestines and help him digest his food. *Communication must become total and conscious before we can stop it.*"

   This problematic is in part the essence of Charles Amirkhanian's radiophonic work, *Andas*. *Andas* (the Swedish word for "breathing") begins with a yoga breathing exercise to aid in sleeping. (It thus stands within the rare genre of artworks created as soporific devices, most notably Bach's *Goldberg Variations*, written to assuage the melancholia that caused the sleepless nights of the Baron von Kayserling.) This sound is soon transformed into snores (eventually resembling a lion's roar), "suspenseful" electronic tones, distorted and disarticulated words in an unrecognizable language, parodies of doowop singing, and finally nonsense chants. This series of vocal transfigurations provides a uniquely radiophonic solution to the problems posed by a radical reconstitution of the body in modernist audio art.

6. Valère Novarina, "Each Word is a Drama," trans. Allen S. Weiss, in *Nonsense: Culture Through the Looking Glass,* a special issue of *Art & Test,* edited by David Allison, John Hanhardt, Mark Roberts, Allen S. Weiss, no. 37 (1990): 75.
7. Douglas Kahn, "Track Organology," *October* 55 (1991).
8. "Each Word Is a Drama," p. 75.
9. In Gregory Whitehead's radiophonic recording, *Dead Letters,* there are a certain number of disarticulatory intercuts he calls *wounds,* functionally not unlike the violent kitchen cutting interruptions mark off the phrasing of Susan Stone's radio work, *Langue Étude*. (Stone collaborated in the production of *Dead Letters*.) These cuts, after being an immediate textual rupture, are a metaphor of the recording process of editing. It is not by accident that *Dead Letters* begins with both a discussion of the transformation of the form of Napoleon's signature *and* of the monetary value of Napoleon's postmortem castrated member, as Napoleon was a product of the French revolution, connoting that the French, as Novarina reminded us, are cutters of heads. (See Valère Novarina, "Travailler pour l'incertain; aller sur la mer; passer sur une planche," interview with Philippe Di Meo, *L'Infini* 19 [1987]: 201.)
10. Glenn Gould, "The Prospects of Recording" [1966], *The Glenn Gould Reader* (New York: Alfred A. Knopf, 1984), p. 345.
11. Ibid., p. 333.
12. Ibid., p. 340. We should note that this perfectability is certainly attainable. As Gould has demonstrated in several experiments, it is practically impossible to locate a properly made splice by listening for an error; it can more likely be located by listening for a *too perfect* articulation in a difficult passage.
13. Ibid., p. 348. The diametrical opposite of such splicing to create ideal sound configurations obtains in a work of *bruitage* such as John Cage's *Imaginary Landscape #4*. This piece for twelve radios—a do-it-yourself composition determined by chance operations of the *I Ching*—demands two operators per radio, controlling changes of amplitude from *ppppp* to *sfffffz,* of frequency settings spanning the dial, and of duration. It was first performed in 1951, at the McMillan Theater at Columbia University, "conducted" by Cage himself. But due to awkward scheduling, it didn't occur until 11:30 P.M., an hour at which, in that epoch, there was practi-

cally nothing on the radio. The result seemed to some an unfortunate mix of static and silence, yet others recognized it as the most fortunate serendipity, prefiguring Cage's inventions of the use of silence in musical composition. (True to form, Cage claimed that he had indeed foreseen the fragility of this work and that the radios performed perfectly that evening. See his statement in *For the Birds: John Cage in Conversation with Daniel Charles* [Boston: Marion Boyers Inc., 1981], p. 169.) This attempt at a noisy collage of music, voice, and the assorted sounds of commercial radio—a music created with radiophonic detritus—like the later *William's Mix*, was possible by the radical consideration of the radio as active musical agent and not merely as a passive transmitter.

14. Cited in Mary Ann Doane, "Ideology and the Practice of Sound Editing and Mixing," in *The Cinematic Apparatus*, ed. Teresa de Lauretis and Stephen Heath (London: Macmillan, 1980), p. 54.
15. Antonin Artaud, "Fragments d'un journal d'enfer" [1926], in *Oeuvres Complètes* I* (Paris: Gallimard, 1984), p. 117. All further references to Artaud will be cited in parenthesis, referring to the Gallimard edition.
16. This shock-counter shock model was suggested to me by Gregory Whitehead.
17. On the acousmetric voice in the cinema, see Michel Chion, *La voix au cinéma* (Paris: Éditions de l'Étoile, 1982); pp. 25–33.
18. Antonin Artaud, "To Have Done with the Judgement of God," trans. Clayton Eshleman and Norman Glass, *Antonin Artaud: Four Texts* (Los Angeles: Panjandrum Books, 1982), p. 79.
19. Roman Jakobson, *Six Lectures on Sound and Meaning*, trans. John Mepham (Cambridge, Mass.: M.I.T. Press, 1978), p. 6.
20. Ivan Fónagy, *La vive voix* (Paris: Payot, 1983), p. 89.
21. Ibid., p. 112.
22. See Allen S. Weiss, "K," in *A+T* [*Art & Text*] 37 (1990): 56–59.
23. For an autobiographical rationale of Whitehead's fascination with the radiophonic transformation of the body, see his "The Forensic Theater: Memory Plays for The Post-Mortem Condition," *Performing Arts Journal* 35–36 (1990); see also Whitehead's "Wrong Side Out," *Lusitania* 3, (1990). On the representation of pain, see Elaine Scarry, *The Body in Pain* (Oxford: Oxford University Press, 1985).
24. Travailler pour l'incertain, p. 205.
25. Valère Novarina, *Le drame de la vie* (Paris, P.O.L., 1984); p. 9. See also Valère Novarina's working notes to *Le drame de la vie*, "Imperatives," trans. Allen S. Weiss, and "Indicatives," my introduction to this work, both in *Sulfur* #27, 1990.
26. Valère Novarina, *Vous qui habitez le temps* (Paris: P.O.L., 1989), p. 19.
27. "Travailler pour l'incertain," p. 200.

CHAPTER 11. KINOMADNESS

1. René Descartes, *Les météores* ("Discours Huitième: De l'arc-en-ciel"), *Oeuvres et lettres* (Paris: Gallimard/Pléiade, 1953), pp. 230–244.
2. See Jurgis Baltrušaitus, *Le miroir* (Paris: Éditions in Elmayan and Éditions du Seuil, 1978), passim.
3. See Jean-François Lyotard's "L'acinéma," *Des dispositifs pulsionnels* (Paris: U.G.E. 10/18, 1973), for a treatment of the relations between pyrotechnics and cinema.
4. Villiers de l'Isle-Adam, "L'affichage céleste" [1873], *Contes cruels* (Paris: Gallimard, 1983); on the role of Villier de l'Isle-Adam's *L'Eve future* in relation to this problematic, see Annette Michelson, "On the Eve of the Future: The Reasonable Facsimile and the Philosophical Toy," *October* 29 (1984).
5. See Allan Sekula, "The Body and the Archive," *October* 39 (1986); and Danielle Duval, "In This Dense Democracy," *Art & Text* 23–24 (1987).
6. Sekula, ibid., p. 55.
7. *The New English Bible* (Oxford and Cambridge: Oxford and Cambridge University Presses, 1970), p. 320. We should note that the metaphor used to describe these events is incorrect. Though the section of *Revelations* describing them is entitled "The Opening of the Sealed Books," the events are in fact described visually; if it is a book that is in question, it would take the form of an illuminated manuscript. The terror and iconography of such an apocolypse was not lost on the cinematic imagination. In 1916, Blaise Cendrars wrote a screenplay entitled *The End of the World Filmed by the Angel of Notre Dame,* which was to have been a remake of the *Book of Revelation* starring Charlie Chaplin. For a partial English translation by Esther Allen and Monique Chefdor, see *Sulfur* 28 (1991), pp. 187–195.
8. Ibid., p. 322.
9. Hans Prinzhorn, *Artistry of the Mentally Ill,* pp. 159–160.
10. Note Abel Gance's pioneering use of extremely brief, fast-action and quick-cut segments; or much later, Robert Breer's utilization of single-frame work. On an instance of the theological subtext in an avant-garde film and the role of God as a mystical movie-projector, see Allen S. Weiss, "Frampton's Lemma, Zorn's Dilemma," in *October* 32 (1985).
11. Peter Stallybrass and Allon White, *The Politics and Poetics of Transgression* (Ithaca, N.Y.: Cornell University Press, 1986), pp. 174–176.
12. Octave Mannoni, "Writing and Madness," in *Psychosis and Sexual Identity: Toward a Post-Analytic View of the Schreber Case,* p. 58.

13. Max Ernst, "Au-délà de la peinture" [1936], *Écritures* (Paris: Gallimard, 1970), p. 256.
14. Ibid., p. 269.
15. Ibid., pp. 241–242; See also Jurgis Baltrušaitus, *Aberrations* (Paris: Flammarion, 1983), especially the chapter on "Pierres imagées."
16. Ibid., 245; see the list of Ernst's hallucinations cited in this text.
17. Ibid., p. 253. A fascinating example manifesting such a marine, or in this case perhaps divine, whisky is that of the contemporary artist J. B. Murry, a Fundamentalist black American creator of Outsider Art. Murry believed that his works (comprosed mainly of thick brush-strokes with two dots serving as "eyes" to physiognomize and orient the image) and writing (pure, illegible glossographia) were directly inspired by God. He claimed that to properly see his works, one had to look through a small water-filled bottle, which he constantly had at his side. To thus observe his drawings is to observe the anamorphic distortion of nearly abstract images—distortions of distortions. See the catalogue to the exhibition *Portraits From the Outside*.
18. Ibid.
19. It is at this juncture that the position of Deleuze and Guattari in *L'Anti-Oedipe* is relevant. Whatever its theoretical difficulties, it at least teaches us to *read* such liminal works as those of Schreber and Artaud *before* undertaking their critical and theoretical dissection.
20. Another related work is Michael Snow's *Flight Stop* (1979), which consists of a flock of sixty fiberglass geese with applied photographs, suspended from the ceiling of a Toronto shopping mall in various postures of flight. This work, which is photography as sculpture as protocinema, harkens back to the origins of cinema, where the visual stop-motion experiments of Étienne Jules Marey and Eadweard Muybridge resulted in a chronophotographic representation of the decomposition of motion. This decomposition marks precisely the articulation of image and narrative. See, Allen S. Weiss, "Lucid Intervals: Postmodernism and Photography," in *Continental Philosophy III: Postmodernism—Philosophy and the Arts*, ed. Hugh Silverman (London: Routledge, 1990).
21. Notably Daniel Paul Schreber's *Memoirs of My Nervous Illness*. Specifically, Smith referred to the film's first tableau as "Schreber's heaven." Furthermore, the film's central figure (the magus who seems to control the action) is derived from *Medical Indoor Exercises* by Daniel Gottlob Moritz Schreber, Daniel Paul's father. The imagery from his father's book, as well as the fact that his father used his posture correcting mech-

anisms on the young Daniel Paul, played a great role in the content (as well as perhaps in the cause) of the paranoid schizophrenic hallucinations of Schreber *fils*.

22. All information on *Heaven and Earth Magic* and citations of Harry Smith are from P. Adams Sitney, *Visionary Film* (Oxford: Oxford University Press, 1979), pp. 249–261.
23. Prinzhorn, *Artistry of the Mentally Ill*, p. 160.
24. Jacques Lacan, "The Mirror Stage as Formative of the Function of the I as Revealed in Psychoanalytic Experience," *Écritis*, trans. Alan Sheridan (New York: Norton, 1981), pp. 4–5. On the problem of projection and identification, see also Sami-Ali, *Corps réel, Corps imaginaire* (Paris: Dunod, 1984).
25. Cited in Joan Copjec, "The Anxiety of the Influencing Machine," *October* 23 (1982): 54. Copjec's article is an excellent Lacanian account of the implications of the psychoanalytic theory of psychosis for film theory.

    We might speculate that if (as so much contemporary film theory insists) the cinematic apparatus indeed consists of not only the physical filmic mechanisms, but also the spectatorial and production "apparatus," then film criticism and theory would also enter directly into this system, into "the apparatus." In that case, it would not be at all strange to consider certain theoretical positions dealing with representation—such as those of Guy Debord, Jean-Louis Baudry, Louis Althusser, and Laura Mulvey, among others—as manifesting the "paranoid" fringes of theory.
26. Sitney, *Visionary Film*, pp. 253, 256.
27. Antonin Artaud, "Sorcellerie et cinéma," *Oeuvres complètes*, vol. 3 (Paris: Gallimard, 1970), p. 83.

CHAPTER 12. EDIBLE ARCHITECTURE, CANNIBAL ARCHITECTURE

1. On the problematic, see Anthony Vidler, "The Architecture of the Uncanny: The Unhomely Houses of the Romantic Sublime," *Assemblage* 3 (1987), 11–14 and passim.
2. Gaston Bachelard, *La terre et les rêveries du repos* (Paris: José Corti, 1948), passim.
3. This film version, created in 1986, was performed by the Pacific Northwest Ballet.
4. The drawing described here is to be found in the collection of the Galerie Alphonse Chave, in Vence, France. On his work, see Luc Debraine, "Eugène Gabritschevsky," *L'Art Brut* Fascicule 16 (Lausanne: Collection de

l'Art Brut, 1990). On the relations between physiognomy, psychopathology, and the grotesque, see Jean-Jacques Courtine, "Raw Bodies" in *Portraits From the Outside: Figurative Expression in Outsider Art,* pp. 37–42, passim.

5. Salvador Dali, "De la beauté terrifiante et comestible de l'architecture modern style," *Minotaure* 3–4 (1933): 68–76.
6. Jean Rousset, *Le Miroir enchanté,* cited in Gérard Genette, *Figures I* (Paris: Seuil, 1966), p. 28.
7. Dali, "De la beauté . . .," p. 28.
8. Jean-Claude Bonnet, "Carême ou les derniers feux de la cuisine décorative," *Romantisme: Revue du Dix-Neuvième Siècle,* vol. 17–18 (Paris: Champion, 1977), p. 40.
9. Ibid., pp. 23–43.
10. Carême, *Le Pâtissier Parisien,* Fourth Part, p. 43; cited in Bonnet, ibid., p. 40.
11. See the recent catalogue of the exhibition *Les Vanités dans la peinture au XVIIe siècle* (Paris: Petit Palais, 1991).
12. See *The Arcimboldo Effect: Transformations of the Face from the 16th to the 20th Century,* ed. Pontus Hulten (New York: Abbeville, 1987).
13. Chantal Thomas, *Casanova: Un voyage libertin* (Paris: Denoël, 1985); p. 145.
14. Marcel Duchamp, *Dialogues with Marcel Duchamp by Pierre Cabanne,* trans. Ron Padgett (New York: Viking, 1971), p. 67. For a study of these works in the context of Duchamp's later production, see Dalia Judovitz, "(Non)sense and (Non)art in Duchamp," in *Nonsense, Art & Text* 37, (1990) 80–86, passim.
15. James Joyce, *Ulysses* [1914] (New York: Random House, 1961), p. 484.
16. See Lisa Phillips, *Frederick Kiesler* (New York: The Whitney Museum and W. W. Norton, 1989).
17. Victor Hugo, *Les travailleurs de la mer* [1866], *Oeuvres complètes: Roman III* (Paris: Laffont, 1985) p. 51: cited in Vidler, "The Architecture of the Uncanny," p. 23.

SELECT BIBLIOGRAPHY

"Les Amants de la langue Autre: Travaux sur le bilinguisme, les glossolalies, la langue étrangère" and "Collubet: Les glossolalies, les psychoses, la psychanalyse des enfants," special issues of *Le Discours Psychanalytique* 6 and 7, 1983.

L'Aracine, the catalogue of L'Aracine, the Musée d'Art Brut at Neuilly-sur-Marne, France, 1988, ed. Madeleine Lommel, Michel Nedjar, Claire Teller.

Antonin Artaud: Dessins et portraits, ed. Paule Thévenin and Jacques Derrida. Paris: Gallimard, 1986.

L'Art Brut, originally the publication of Dubuffet's Compagnie de l'Art Brut, now published by the Collection de l'Art Brut, Lausanne, ed. Michel Thévoz and Geneviève Roulin, vols. 1–16:

1. The Prisoner of Basel, Palanc, The Postman Lonné, Miguel Hernandez, Heinrich Anton Müller.
2. Adolf Wölfli, by W. Morgenthaler (1921).
3. Augustin Lesage, Maisonneuve, The Collection of Dr. Charles Ladame.
4. Scottie Wilson, Guillaume, Paul End.
5. Joseph Crépin, Gaston The Zoologist.
6. Carlo, Laure.
7. Aloïse, by Jacqueline Porret-Forel.
8. Jeanne Tripier.
9. Madge Gill, Émile Ratier, The Collection of Dr. A. Marie.
10. Jules Doudin, Vojislav Jakić.
11. Sylvain Fusco, Aloïs Wey, Carlo's last years.
12. Gugging: Johann Hauser, Philipp Schöpke, August Walla, Oswald Tschirtner, Johann Garber, Max.
13. Reinhold Metz, by Michel Thévoz.
14. Josef Wittlich, Willem van Genk, Hans Krüsi.
15. Giovanni Battista Podestà, by Lucienne Peiry.
16. Yanko Domsic, Eugène Gabritschevsky, Ted Gordon, Benjamin Bonjour, Michel Nedjar.

L'Art brut et après, ed. Gérard Preszow. Brussels: Art en Marge, 1988.

Art Brut: Madness and Marginalia, a special issue of *Art & Text* 27, ed. Allen S. Weiss (1988).

L'Art Fou: de l'art des fous à la folie de l'art, ed. Jean-Pierre Klein; *Art et thérapie* 30/31 (1989).

Bild und Seele: Über Art Brut und Outsider-Kunst, ed. Paolo Bianchi; *Kunstforum* 101 (1989).

André Blavier. *Les fous littéraires*. Paris: Henri Veyrier, 1982.

Les Bulletins d'Art en Marge, vols. 1–32, ed. Françoise Henrion. Brussels: Galerie Art en Marge, 1986–1992.

Roger Cardinal. *Outsider Art*. New York: Prager, 1972.

Laurent Danchin, *Jean Dubuffet: Peintre-philosophe*. Paris: La manufacture, 1988.

Degenerate Art: The Fate of the Avant-Garde in Nazi Germany, ed. Stephanie Barron. Los Angeles: Los Angeles County Museum of Art, 1991.

Jean Dubuffet. *Asyphyxiating Culture*. [1968] Reprinted: Paris: Minuit, 1986. English translation by Carol Volk, *Asphyxiating Culture and Other Writings*. New York: Four Walls Eight Windows, 1988.

———. *Bâtons rompus*. [1980]. Reprinted: Paris: Minuit, 1986.

———. *Prospectus et tous écrits suivants*, vols. 1 and 2. Paris: Gallimard, 1967.

Jean Dubuffet and Art Brut, ed. Thomas Messer and Fred Licht, catalogue to the 1986 exhibition at the Peggy Guggenheim Collection in Venice.

Écrits Bruts, ed. Michel Thévoz. Paris: P.U.F., 1979.

European Outsiders. New York: Rosa Esman Gallery, 1986.

"Les glossolalies," a special issue of *Langages* 91, ed. Jean-Jacques Courtine (Paris, 1988).

The HAI Collection of Outsider Art, 1980–1990, ed. Elizabeth Marks and Thomas Klocke. New York, Hospital Audiences Inc., 1990.

The Heart of Creation: The Art of Martin Ramirez, ed. Elsa Longhauser. Philadelphia: Moore College of Art, 1986.

Heavenly Visions: The Art of Minnie Evans, ed. Mitchell D. Kahan. Raleigh: The North Carolina Museum of Art, 1986.

In Another World: Outsider Art from Europe and America, ed. Monika Kinley. London: The South Bank Center, 1987.

In the Realms of the Unreal, ed. John G.H. Oakes. New York: Four Walls Eight Windows, 1991.

Les jardiniers de la mémoire. Bègles, France: Galerie Imago, 1989.

Rosemarie Koczÿ. Cologne: Galerie Susanne Zander, 1989.

Ernst Kris. *Psychoanalytic Explorations in Art*. New York: International Universities Press, 1952.

Künstler aus Gugging: Zur Art Brut der Gegenwart. Oldenberg: Bibliotheks- und Informationssystem der Universität Oldenberg, 1989.

Jean-Jacques Lecercle. *Philosophy Through the Looking-Glass: Language, nonsense, desire*. La Salle, IL: Open Court, 1985.

Augustin Lesage, 1876–1954. Paris: Philippe Sers Éditeur, 1988.

La linguistique fantastique, ed. Sylvain Aurous *et alia*. Paris: Denoël, 1985.

John MacGregor. *The Discovery of the Art of the Insane*. Princeton: Princeton University Press, 1989.

George Melly. *It's All Writ Out for You: The Life and Work of Scotty Wilson*. London: Thames & Hudson, 1986.

Muffled Voices: Folk Artists in Contemporary America, ed. Didi Barrett. New York: Paine Weber Art Gallery, 1986.

Leo Navratil. *August Walla: Sein Leben & seine Kunst*. Nördlingen: Greno, 1988.

———. *Johann Hauser: Kunst aus Maine und Depression.* Munich: Rogner & Bernhard, 1978.

———. *Schizophrenie und Kunst.* Munich: Deutschen taschenbuch Verlag Gmbh & Co. KG, 1965.

———. *Über schizophrenie und die Federzeichnungen des Patienten O.T..* Munich: Deutschen taschenbuch Verlag Gmbh & Co. KG, 1974.

Michel Nedjar: Arbeiten 1991. Cologne: Galerie Susanne Zander, 1991.

Michel Nedjar: Sculptures "Chair d'Ame". Paris: Galerie Le Gall Peyroulet, 1991.

"Nonsense", a special dossier in *A+T [Art & Text]* 37, ed. David B. Allison, John G. Hanhardt, Mark S. Roberts and Allen S. Weiss, 1990.

The Other Side of the Moon: The World of Adolf Wölfli, ed. Elsa Longhauser and Elka Spoerri. Philadelphia: Moore College of Art, 1988.

Outside USA, vols. 1 and 2, ed. Paolo Bianchi, *Kunstforum* 112 and 113 (Cologne, 1991).

Outsider Art in Australia, ed. Ulli Beier and Philip Hammial. *Aspect* 35, 1989.

Outsider Art from Europe, ed. Sal Scalora. Storrs: The University of Connecticut, 1988.

Outsiders: An Art Without Precedent or Tradition, ed. Roger Cardinal and Victor Musgrave. London: Arts Council of Great Britain, 1979.

Parallel Visions: Modern Artists and Outsider Art, ed. Maurice Tuchman, Carol Eliel, *et alia.* Los Angeles: Los Angeles County Museum of Art, 1992.

Michel Pierssens. *The Power of Babel: A Study of Logophilia,* trans. Carl. R. Lovitt. London: Routledge & Kegan Paul, 1980.

Pioneers in Paradise: Folk and Outsider Artists of the West Coast, ed. Susan Larsen-Martin and Robert Martin. Long Beach, California: Long Beach Gallery of Art, 1985.

Monique Plaza. *Écriture et folie*. Paris: P.U.F., 1986.

Portraits From the Outside: Figurative Expression in Outsider Art, ed. Simon Carr, Betsey Farber, Sam Farber and Allen S. Weiss. New York: The Parsons School of Design, 1990.

Hans Prinzhorn. *Artistry of the Mentally Ill* [1922]. English translation: Berlin: Springer-Verlag, 1968.

The Prinzhorn Collection, ed. Stephen Prokopoff. Champaign: The Krannert Art Gallery, 1984.

Martin Ramierz, ed. Robert Littman. Mexico City: Centro Cultural Arte, 1988.

Raw Vision, ed. John Maizels, a journal of Outsider Art, Art Brut, Grassroots Art, Contemporary Folk Art, Visionary Art.

Daniel Paul Schreber. *Memoirs of My Nervous Illness* [1903], trans. Ida Macalpine and Richard A. Hunter. Cambridge, Massachusetts: Harvard University Press, 1988.

Nisa da Silveira. *Imagens do inconsciente*. Rio de Janeiro: Alhambra, 1981.

Sonneastro: Die Künstler aus Gugging; Medium #11 (Vienna, 1990), ed. Johann Feilacher.

Susan Stewart. *Nonsense*. Baltimore: Johns Hopkins University Press, 1988.

Michel Thévoz. *Art Brut*, trans. James Emmons. New York: Rizzoli, 1976.

———. *Art Brut, psychose et médiumité*. Paris: Éditions de la Différence, 1990.

———. *Art, folie, graffiti, LSD, etc*. Switzerland, Éditions de l'Aire, 1985.

———. *Détournement d'écriture*. Paris: Minuit, 1989.

———. Dubuffet. Geneva: Skira, 1986.

———. *Le langage de la rupture*. Paris: P.U.F., 1978.

———. *Louis Soutter*. Lausanne: L'Age d'Homme, 1989.

Transmitters: The Isolate Artist in America, ed. Elsa Linghauser. Philadelphia: Moore College of Art, 1981.

Adolf Wölfli, ed. Elka Spoerri and Jürgen Glaesemer. Bern: The Adolf Wölfli Foundation, 1976.

Adolf Wölfli: Dessinateur-Compositeur, ed. Geneviève Roulin, Elka Spoerri and Michel Thévoz. Lausanne: L'Age d'Homme, 1991.

Louis Wolfson. *Ma mère, musicienne, est morte . . .* Paris: Navarin, 1984.

Louis Wolfson. *Le schizo et les langues*. Paris: Gallimard, 1970.-